CALDECOTT Activity BOOK

Caldecott Activity Book

© 2007 Claudia Krause

To be used with *Kitten's First Full Moon*, by Kevin Henkes

Dedication, Acknowledgments, Art credits

A special thank you to Kevin Henkes, the author of *Kitten's First Full Moon*, and Harper Collins Publishing Company for publishing this delightful story.

Dedication

This book is dedicated to the memory of my mother, father, and brother. Their love for life and learning inspired me in untold ways.

INTRODUCTION

Welcome to a story adventure. The enclosed questions and activities for this delightful book can be used by parents, grandparents, guardians, and teachers. The book can be read at any time of the year, allowing the reader to make different choices from the activity book with each reading. The questions and activities are not numbered, which allows the reader ownership of the questions, activities, and timeline.

The questions are designed to develop critical thinking, vocabulary, math skills, as well as science knowledge, all while deepening the children's understanding of a wonderful story. The activities foster creativity and individual expression, offering various art, writing, and research opportunities. The activities can be done at home with parents, grandparents, or guardians, or they can be used by teachers in the classroom. Teachers can use the questions and activities as class assignments, homework assignments, or learning center activities. Create a reading center in the classroom or at home, and provide baskets of books about cats, the moon, space, and gravity. Provide pillows, carpet squares, or animal beds, where the children can sit comfortably.

I encourage parents, grandparents, or guardians to take their children to the local library, where they can explore age-appropriate materials related to the activities. Research suggestions are offered throughout the activity book, and most libraries have computers available for children to use. Ask the librarian to suggest additional age-appropriate websites.

I suggest visiting various community locations. It only takes a phone call to inquire about available enrichment opportunities. Many businesses are willing to allow children to visit their facilities, offering guided tours, as well as information. Call these businesses to find out what opportunities might be available. Additionally, contacts with professional organizations may also be fruitful. I suggest that teachers contact their local school district to obtain a list of organizations that are willing to enrich the educational experiences of children. Some of these organizations are happy to contribute to special projects and field trips, thus furthering the children's academic knowledge.

I'd love to see how you've developed the enclosed questions and activities. Please feel free to send me pictures, projects, ideas, samples, suggestions, and your responses to the material. I will try to disseminate your ideas to others. I hope you have a wonderful experience reading this book and doing the activity package. Happy learning!

TEXT: Kitten's First ...

> Direct the children's attention to the front cover. Encourage them to answer the following questions in complete sentences.

The [ ] around the text indicate a question.

- **[What do you see on the front cover?]** (See Art section below.)

- **[Is it daytime or nighttime? How do you know?]**

- **[Why do you think Kitten is out at night?]**

- **[What is Kitten doing on the front cover?]** (e.g., She's licking her paw.)

- SAY: Many animals are considered pets, including kittens and cats. Raise your hand if you have a pet.

- SAY: They're "family members." Their owners and family care for them. **[Do you think it's a good idea to allow animals to go outside at night? Why or why not?]**

- **[Why is Kitten licking herself?]** (e.g., She's probably cleaning herself.) (See Science section below.)

- SAY: Kitten is a cat. **[What do you know about cats?]**

> Create a KWL chart. (Things I _Know_ about cats/kittens, Things I _Want_ to learn about cats/kittens, and Things I _Learned_ about cats/kittens.) Draw three boxes on a piece of paper and write the three statements listed below in each box. Write the children's responses in each box. Place the chart in a location where they can add additional information as they discover new facts. (To be placed in chart with three boxes.)

What I Know About Cats	What I Want To Know About Cats	What I Learned About Cats
• I know cats have ears. • I know cats have claws.	• I want to know if cats have good hearing. • I want to know if cats have a good sense of smell.	• There are many different types of cats.

6

Go to www.scienceforkids/kittenfacts.com, and read additional information about kittens to the children. They will enjoy hearing some of the interesting things listed on this site.

- SAY: The moon is behind Kitten. **[What do you know about the moon?]**

> **Create a KWL chart. (Things I _Know_ about the moon, Things I _Want_ to learn about the moon, and Things I _Learned_ about the moon.) See the previous example about kittens/cats. They can add to this chart as they discover new facts.**

Go to www.scienceforkids/moonfacts.com, and read additional information about the moon to the children. They can add additional information to the KWL chart.

- **[What do you think Kitten thinks about the moon?]** (See Writing section below.)

ACTIVITIES

The brackets [ ] around the text indicate a question.

Art

Have the children recreate the front cover of the book. Have them trace around a circular template onto a piece of white or yellow construction paper, cutting around the circle to represent the moon. (See Resource section at the end of the book.) Have them glue the moon onto a piece of black construction paper. On another piece of paper, have the children paint or draw Kitten, licking her paw. Allow it to dry. Have them cut around Kitten, gluing it to the lower portion of the moon. A small piece of pink felt, representing her tongue, could be glued onto the picture. This shows Kitten licking her paw. Have the children color or paint different flowers on a separate piece of paper, cutting around each flower and gluing it to the lower portion of the page.

Writing

- **[What do you think Kitten thinks about the big, white thing in the sky?]**

- **[Do you think Kitten even notices that it's there?]**

- **[What do you think Kitten might say about it?]** (e.g., That big round thing in the sky is beautiful. I wish I could stalk bugs on it.)

> **Write the children's responses on a piece of paper and have them copy one sentence. If they'd like to write their own sentence, be available to help them sound out the correct spelling of the words. Put their writing next to their front cover picture.**

Science

- SAY: Kitten is using her tongue to lick her paw. **[Have you ever looked at your tongue?]**

Distribute a small mirror to each child, cautioning them to be very careful with the mirror. Have them examine their tongue. Then, have the children sit with a partner, examining each other's tongue. Talk about appropriate behaviors during this experience, emphasizing that scientists observe important details in people and nature. Tell them that making inappropriate tongue gestures will not be acceptable. Direct their attention to the little bumps that are on the surface of the tongue. Explain to them that Kitten also has these small bumps on her tongue.

- **[Do you know what these little bumps do?]**

Allow the children to relay what they think the bumps do. Tell the children that they allow us to taste and they're called *taste buds*. Explain that the entire tongue can detect different tastes, but some areas are more sensitive to certain tastes than others. Go to www.scienceforkids/tongue.com and show them the picture of the tongue. It shows the taste buds appearing on the surface of the tongue. Explain to the children that the taste buds detect certain tastes.

Give each child a copy of the tongue. (See Resource section.) Have the children examine their tongue again with the mirror, drawing the taste buds appearing there. Have the www.scienceforkids/tongue.com website available for the children to see, as well as books from the library. Collect the mirrors after they've drawn the taste buds and place them in a secure location.

After the children have drawn the taste buds on the tongue, have them experiment with the sweet, sour, salty, bitter, and savory substances. (See below.) A tub should be placed between two children with the following items inside the tub. Small jars containing a small amount of the sweet, sour, salty, bitter, and savory substances. A small plastic bag filled with cotton swabs. Two plastic cups, filled halfway with water. The cups should have the child's name written on the front, so they don't drink from each other's cup. Two empty cups, with the child's name written on the front should be placed inside the tub, so they can spit the contents of the taste test into their individual cups.

The teacher/adult can do the following tongue experiment individually, in small groups, in a learning center, or as a class experience. Parental permission is needed for this experiment, as some children might be allergic to the substances used. (See parent permission letter in the Resource section.) If the teacher feels more comfortable doing the experiment with one child at a time, this can be accomplished on successive days. If this experiment is done as a class, tell the children that appropriate behavior is required. This means that the tubs they will be receiving are not to be moved, that they must listen to all directions, and the cotton swabs that are inside the plastic bag can only be dipped into the jars once at each end, as it will touch the surface of their tongue. The used cotton swabs are to be placed in the bottom of the tub, and they are not to be touched or used again. The teacher should demonstrate the proper way to dip both ends of the cotton swab into the jar and touch different parts of the tongue. The teacher should also demonstrate how to rinse the mouth; sipping a small amount of water, circulating it inside the mouth, and carefully spitting the water into their individual plastic cup. Their cups must be placed in a location that will not spill. Two pencils should also be placed inside the tub, as they will need to mark the location of the sweet, sour, salty, bitter, and savory taste on the tongue page.

Mix and label the following substances, placing them in small jars. Mix as many batches as needed for the entire class.

1. Sweet: ¼ cup water, mixed with 2 tablespoons of sugar.
   Sour: several tablespoons of lemon juice.
   Salty: ¼ cup water, mixed with 2 tablespoons of salt.
   Bitter: several tablespoons of cold, strong coffee.
   Savory: several tablespoons of soy sauce, or crushed tomatoes.

2. If the children want to work with a partner, have them choose a partner. The partners will share a tub.

3. Place the five jars containing the various substances inside their plastic tub. Write each child's name on the front of a plastic cup and partially fill the cup with water. This will allow them to rinse their tongue during the experiment. In addition, write each child's name on the front of an empty plastic cup and place these inside their tub. This will allow them to discard the water inside their mouth. Place small mirrors inside their plastic tub.

   Run off copies of the tongue page. (See Resource section.) Place ten tongue pages inside a folder for each pair to use. The folders should be placed outside the tub, so they don't get wet. The children will need to get these pages from the folder after each experiment, so they need to decide where they'll put their folder. Each child will need to label the top of the tongue pages as Sweet, Sour, Salty, Bitter, and Savory during the experiment. They will be marking an "X" on the location(s) on the tongue where they tasted these substances. Have them use the pencils inside the tub for this purpose.

4. The teacher or adult should write the word SWEET on a piece of paper. SAY: Let's say the letters together. (e.g. S-W-E-E-T.) Tell the children to point to the small jar inside their tub with the same letters. Make sure they point to the SWEET jar. When you're sure that they've identified the correct jar, ask them to take one cotton swab from the plastic bag and carefully dip one end into the SWEET jar. Using the mirror that was placed inside their tub, have them look at their tongue and carefully touch several spots on their tongue. **[Did you taste the SWEET substance on any part of your tongue?]** Have them dip the opposite end of the cotton swab into the SWEET jar a second time and repeat the process. Have them discard the cotton swab in one corner of the tub. **[Did you find a place on your tongue where the SWEET taste was very strong?]** We're going to mark that place on your tongue page.

5. Have the children get a tongue page from their folder. Have them take a pencil from the tub and write the word SWEET on the top of the page. Now, have them put an "X" on the location(s) of the tongue where the SWEET taste was very strong. Ask the children to carefully take a few sips of water from their cup and swirl it around in their mouth. Then, have them spit this water into their empty cup. Emphasize to the children that they need to place their cups in a location that will be safe.

6. Repeat this process for the other four substances.

7. Ask the children what they learned from this experiment. Write their comments on a piece of paper. (e.g., I learned that the tongue has little bumps on it. These bumps help us taste sweet, sour, salty, things, etc.) Ask them to copy one of the comments and staple their tongue pages to the back of their comment(s) page.

They should discover that some areas of their tongue are more sensitive to the various tastes. **[Did everyone taste the sweet taste at the same place?] [What happened when you placed the cotton swab with the sweet substance on different portions of your tongue?]** The children should come to the realization that the tongue can taste the sweet taste in several locations on the tongue. There isn't a single location for this taste, but the sweet receptors are located throughout the tongue.

Have the children go to www.scienceforkids/tongue.com to find out additional information about the tongue. Have them write down several facts that they learned, relaying these facts to a friend or the class. They can staple these facts to their Tongue Page.

TEXT: Kitten's First...

> **Direct the children's attention to the copyright page. Encourage them to answer the following questions in compete sentences.**

The [ ] around the text indicate a question.

- **[What do you see on this page?] [What do the details on this page tell you about the story?]** (e.g., That there's a full moon in the sky and it might be Kitten's first full moon.)

- **[How would you describe Kitten on this page?]** (e.g., Well, she seems relaxed, etc.)

ACTIVITIES

The [ ] around the text indicate a question.

Writing

- SAY: Kitten is sitting outside. **[What do you think she's thinking?]**
  Write the children's responses on a piece of paper.

Have the children review the class responses about what they think Kitten is thinking, and then have them write a few of their own sentences. You should be available to help them sound out the words. (e.g., Wow, that big, round, ball in the sky is very beautiful.)

TEXT: It was...

> **Direct the children's attention to the page where Kitten is on the porch.
> Encourage them to answer the following questions in complete sentences.**

The [ ] around the text indicate a question.

- **[What do you see in the picture?]**

- **[What do you call the flying insects in the sky?]** (e.g., They're called *fireflies* or *lightning bugs*.)

- **[Why are they called *fireflies* or *lightning bugs*?]** (e.g., They're called fireflies because they light up at night.) (See Science section below.)

- **[Do you think Kitten enjoys watching the fireflies?]**

- **[Is Kitten a female or a male cat?]** (e.g., It said, "she" in the text, so it must be a female cat.)

- **[When she saw the moon, what did she think it was?]** (e.g., She thought it was a bowl of milk and she wanted it.)

- **[Why would Kitten think that the moon was a bowl of milk?]** (e.g., It looks like a bowl of milk and she's probably been given milk in a bowl.)

- **[What information could you tell me about Kitten's house?]** (e.g., Well, it has steps to a porch area, it has a railing, and there are flowers planted below the steps.)

- SAY: There are flowers planted below the steps. **[What are your favorite flowers?]** Ask the children to name as many flowers as they can, recording their responses on a piece of paper. (See Art section.)

- SAY: This page said she wanted the "bowl of milk" in the sky. **[What do you think Kitten will do to try to get the "bowl of milk"?] [How do you think she'll try to get it?]** Write the children's responses on a piece of paper.

- **[Have you ever wanted something very badly?]** (See Writing section below.)

- **[What did you do to get what you wanted?]** Write the children's responses on a piece of paper.

ACTIVITIES

The [ ] around the text indicate a question.

Art

Have the children draw or paint some flowers on a piece of white construction paper. Let this dry. Cut around the flowers and glue them to a piece of dark blue or black construction paper.

- **[Do you remember the names of some of the flowers we talked about?]**

Have the children quickly name their favorite flowers. Have a variety of flower books available from the library for the children to examine. Bring a variety of flowers to class for the children to smell and examine. You could even attempt to put the names of various flowers in alphabetical order. (i.e., D – daisy, P – pansy, R – rose, S – sunflower, V – violet, etc.)

Have the children recreate this page by drawing or painting Kitten on the steps. Have them draw or paint fireflies on a piece of white construction paper. Let this dry. Place a circular glue trail under the fireflies and sprinkle gold/yellow glitter onto the glue trail. Let this dry. Cut around the fireflies and glue these onto the page. They might like to cut out a moon to add to their picture.

Writing

- SAY: Kitten wanted the "bowl of milk" she saw in the sky. Brainstorm and write on a piece of paper various things the children might want. (e.g., A class party, a class pet, art supplies, a field trip, etc.) Have them think of ways that they could achieve their goal and write their responses around the brainstormed ideas. (e.g., We could earn a class party by reaching our reading goal. We could earn a field trip by . . .)

Science

Go to www.scienceforkids/fireflies.com and read the facts about the fireflies to the children. **[Which facts were your favorite?]** Write down on a piece of paper the facts they enjoyed hearing. Have them write one of the sentences from the paper. Have them glue this information to the back of their firefly page.

Math

SAY: Raise your hand if you've ever seen a firefly. Let's count the number of children who've seen a firefly. (e.g., Three children have seen a firefly. Five children have never seen a firefly.) Write these numbers on a piece of paper. (e.g., YES - 3, NO - 5, etc.) Have the children practice counting and writing the number of hands raised. If no one has ever seen a firefly, write a 0 on a piece of paper. Have the children practice writing this number on a whiteboard or a piece of paper.

Review the number of children who have/have not seen a firefly. Create a bar graph of the results. (e.g. YES-3, NO-5.) Talk about how a bar graph is created and how it relays important information to the reader. This bar graph represents the number of children who have/have not seen a firefly. It also tells us how many children are in class, because the total number of squares on the graph will equal the number of children in class. Each colored square represents one child. Have the children color the appropriate number of squares on a one-inch grid. (e.g., I have seen a firefly—three children. I have not seen a firefly—five children.)

TEXT: So she...

> **Direct the children's attention to the page where Kitten is trying to catch a firefly with her tongue. Encourage them to answer the following questions in complete sentences.**

The [ ] around the text indicate a question.

- **[What do you see in the picture?]**

- SAY: The author tells us that Kitten "closed her eyes." **[Why did she do this?]**

- **[Do you think closing your eyes helps you think better? Why or why not?]**

Write the word *IMAGINATION* on a piece of paper. **[Does anyone know what this word means?]** Tell the children what the word means. (i.e., This word means "to form new ideas.")

- **[Do you think Kitten has an imagination? Why or why not?]** (e.g., Well, she thinks she can lick the "bowl of milk" with her tongue, so she must have an imagination!)

- **[Have you ever used your imagination?] [How did you use your imagination?]** Write their responses on a piece of paper. (e.g., I used my imagination when I wrote a story. I used my imagination when I fixed my bike, etc.)

- SAY: Kitten tried to lick the "bowl of milk." She was hoping that she could taste it. **[Why wouldn't this be possible?]** (e.g., Kitten's tongue isn't long enough to reach the moon.) The children can find out the distance from the Earth to the moon by doing additional research. Go to www.scienceforkids/moon.com to read this information to the children. (See Science section below.)

- SAY: Kitten has one of her paws raised. **[Which one is it?]** (i.e., Her left paw.) **[How do you know?]** Have the children stand up and face you. Ask them to raise their left hand. If they're not sure, demonstrate by raising your right hand, which would appear as the left hand to them. You could play Simon Says for a few minutes to reinforce the left/right concept. (e.g., Simon says to raise your left hand. Simon says to raise your right hand, etc.)

ACTIVITIES

The [ ] around the text indicate a question.

Art

Have the children draw or paint large fireflies that could be hung from the ceiling. Go to www.scienceforkids/firefly.com to examine the body structure of the firefly. Have them create their own firefly, with green, yellow, or pale red glitter "lights" glued to the end of the body. Let these dry and string them with yarn or fishing line. Hang these from the ceiling, with the glitter side down.

Writing/Oral Language

- SAY: We talked about the word *imagination*. We said we thought that Kitten used her imagination when she stuck out her tongue to lick the "bowl of milk." Review their responses.

- SAY: You have to imagine a thing before you can create or solve a problem. For example, I would need to imagine or think of ways that I could solve the problem of a broken shoelace. I would have to think of ways that I could keep the shoe closed. I might look around my apartment or house for things that I could use to solve my broken shoelace problem. I might see a large rubber band lying on the kitchen table. I could cut it and lace it into my shoe. It might not be the most fashionable article, but it might work. That's using your imagination. **[When have you had to solve a problem, or create something because you needed it?]**

Brainstorm ways that the children might use their imaginations, relaying how they solved the problem. (e.g., A problem with their bike, a toy, a missing homework assignment, lack of space in their room, etc.)

Science

- SAY: The firefly is actually a winged beetle. It can produce a light from its body that is called *bioluminescence*. It's a chemically produced light that can be green, yellow, or pale red. Go online to www.scienceforkids/firefly.com and review the interesting facts about them.

- SAY: It's amazing that the firefly has the ability to create light within its body. This light is produced in a special way within the firefly's body. **[How many of you have seen a glow stick?]** A glow stick works in somewhat the same way. Chemicals come together to produce light. There are two substances in the glow stick. When you break the barrier between the two substances it creates a reaction, which produces light. Fireflies can create this light naturally. Let's watch a glow stick produce a chemical reaction. Demonstrate this reaction with a glow stick.

- SAY: The distance from the Earth to the moon is approximately 238,855 miles. That's a long way. **[How long is a mile?]** Let the children respond and write down their answers. Hold up a ruler and tell them that a ruler equals one foot. A mile would be 5,280 rulers placed end to end. Tell them you don't have enough rulers to measure that far, but a car can travel a mile in a short amount of time. Give the children an idea of how far a mile would be by locating familiar landmarks in their town. (e.g., The distance from the school to the grocery store would be about a mile.) Have them ask their parents, grandparents, or guardians to show them how far a mile would be in a car. If possible, get a pedometer and take the children on a mile walk. They could simply walk around the playground until the pedometer recorded a mile. This might take two days to accomplish, but it would give them an idea of the distance.

Math

- SAY: Kitten raised her left paw on this page. **[Show me which hand you use to write or draw.]** Create a bar graph of the number of children in class who use their left/right hand. Record the number of children who use each hand on a piece of paper. Talk about how a bar graph is created and how it relays important information to the reader. This bar graph represents the number of children who use either their left or right hand to write or draw. It also tells us how many children are in class, because the left/right hand numbers are added together, and they should equal the total number of children in class. Each colored square on the graph represents one child. Have the children color in the appropriate number of squares on a one-inch grid.

WHICH HAND DO YOU USE TO WRITE OR DRAW?

I use my left hand - ■ ■ ■   Left hand = Red

I use my right hand - ■ ■ ■ ■ ■ ■   Right hand = Blue

                                                                One square = one child

TEXT: But Kitten only...

> **Direct the children's attention to the page showing Kitten with a firefly on her tongue. Encourage them to answer the following questions in complete sentences.**

The [ ] around the text indicate a question.

- **[What do you see in the picture?]**

- **[How would you describe the look on Kitten's face?] [Does she look happy?] [Does she look sad?] [How do you know?]** Write the children's responses on a piece of paper. (See Art and Writing sections.)

- **[Why does the bug stick to Kitten's tongue?]** (e.g., The tongue is moist and this moisture made the bug stick.)

- **[Why do you think the firefly doesn't just fly away?]**

- **[How many fireflies are on this page?]** (Answer: There are four fireflies in the sky and one on Kitten's tongue.) **[What is 4 + 1?]** (i.e., 4 + 1 = 5.)

- SAY: There are five fireflies on this page. **[How many ways can you make five?]** (i.e., 0 + 5 = 5, 1 + 4 = 5, 2 + 3 = 5, 3 + 2 = 5, 4 + 1 = 5, etc.) Write these combinations on a piece of paper. (See Math section below.)

- **[Why do you think the author says, "Poor Kitten!"?]**

- **[Do you think Kitten might enjoy eating the firefly? Why or why not?] [What foods does your cat like to eat?]** Write the food choices on a piece of paper.

- SAY: Kitten has raised her paw again. **[Which paw did she raise this time?]** (e.g., She raised her left paw.)

- Review the bar graph the children created earlier about the use of their hands. (e.g., I use my left hand. I use my right hand.) **[Why don't we all use the same hand?]** Allow the children to relay their thoughts. Tell the children that when they first started to write, their brain preferred to use one side.

ACTIVITIES

The [ ] around the text indicate a question.

Art

Have the children illustrate the surprised look on Kitten's face. Have them decide if they want to paint their own surprised look on Kitten's face or if they'd like to glue on large, wiggly eyes. Do the following:

1. Have the children recreate this page by drawing or painting Kitten on a piece of black construction paper. If they choose to glue the wiggly eyes to the picture, tell the children to leave space for them. Draw or paint the five fireflies on a separate piece of paper. Let these dry.

2. Have the children spread a circular glue trail to the bottom of the firefly body and sprinkle with green, yellow, or pale red glitter. Let this dry. Cut these out and glue four of them onto the black construction paper next to Kitten.

3. Cut out a piece of pink felt to represent Kitten's tongue. Have the children glue this to Kitten's mouth. Let this dry.

4. Have the children glue the last firefly onto Kitten's tongue.

5. Have the children cut out a white moon and glue this to their picture.

6. If the children decided to glue the wiggly eyes onto Kitten's face, they can do this now.

Writing

- We talked about the words we could use to describe the look on Kitten's face. She might have been surprised, scared, amazed, shocked, etc. These words are called *synonyms*. Synonyms are words that are similar. We have a special book called a *thesaurus* that helps us find words that are similar.

Show the children a thesaurus and look up one word. (e.g., Surprise.) Write the word on a piece of paper with the synonyms listed next to the word. Have the children write this example, and then orally relay a sentence to a friend. (e.g., I was startled to see Kitten with a firefly stuck on her tongue.)

SURPRISE   **STARTLE**   **SHOCK**   **STUN**

Have the children orally relay some details about Kitten's first experience with the firefly. Write their responses on a piece of paper. (e.g., Kitten was sitting on her porch. She stuck out her wet tongue. A firefly landed on it. Kitten was very surprised. She opened her eyes wide. She didn't know what to do. The firefly felt strange on her tongue. The firefly was probably surprised, too. The firefly thinks it will be eaten, etc.) Explain to the children that writing involves putting our thoughts on paper. Tell them that we decide what we want to say, then we organize our ideas. Show the children the sentences they created and tell them that they're going to put their sentences in order. They're going to create a paragraph about Kitten's experience. Cut the sentences into strips. Do the following:

1. Ask them to think of a good title for the writing. (e.g., Kitten's First Firefly Experience.) Start arranging their sentences in a logical order. (e.g., Kitten was sitting on her porch and she stuck out her wet tongue. A firefly landed on the tip of her tongue. She was very surprised!)

2. Explain to them that we can combine our thoughts and events into a whole paragraph. Explain that a paragraph is a group of sentences that relay these thoughts and events, and when they're combined they make a paragraph. Read the finished paragraph to the children and have them write sentences for a specified period. They could write a few sentences each day until the paragraph is finished.

Math

- SAY: There are five fireflies on this page.

On a piece of paper, write $0 + 5 = 5$, $1 + 4 = 5$. After reviewing the various combinations that equal five, talk about the commutative principle of addition.

Commute means "to move around." I could move the numbers around by writing the addition sentence as $0 + 5 = 5$, or I could write it as $5 + 0 = 5$. They both equal 5. $0+5=5$ and $5+0=5$, $1+4=5$ and $4+1=5$, $2+3=5$ and $3+2=5$.

- **[What do you notice about the first column of numbers shown below?]** (e.g., The numbers are increasing by one number each time.)

- **[What do you notice about the second column of numbers?]** (e.g., The numbers are decreasing by one number each time.)

- **[Do you see that all the numbers add up to 5?]** (e.g., I can move the numbers to different positions, but the answer will still equal 5.)

$$0 + 5 = 5$$
$$1 + 4 = 5$$
$$2 + 3 = 5$$
$$3 + 2 = 5$$
$$4 + 1 = 5$$
$$5 + 0 = 5$$

TEXT: Still, there was...

Direct the children's attention to the page where the full moon is in the sky and the firefly is right next to Kitten. Encourage them to answer the following questions in complete sentences.

The [ ] around the text indicate a question.

- **[What do you see in the picture?]** (See Art section.)

- SAY: The author tells us that the "little bowl" was just waiting. **[What do you think Kitten is thinking and feeling?] [Do you think she's discouraged? Why or why not?] [Have you ever felt discouraged or frustrated?]**

- **[How many fireflies are on this page?]** SAY: Show me with your fingers.

- **[Do you think this is the same firefly that got stuck on Kitten's tongue? Why or why not?]**

- Point to Kitten's whiskers and ask the following question: **[What do we call these things sticking out from Kitten's face?]** (e.g. Whiskers.) (See Art, Science, and Math sections.)

- **[Do you think Kitten's whiskers are important? Why or why not?]** Write the children's responses on a piece of paper.

- **[If Kitten didn't eat the firefly, what do you think the firefly would say to Kitten?] [What do you think Kitten would say to the firefly?]** (See Writing/Oral Language section.)

Create some conversation bubbles on a piece of paper to relay their comments. (See Resource section.) (e.g., Firefly: "Thank you so much for not eating me, I love flying around at night." Kitten: "I didn't want to eat you. I'd rather have a bowl of milk!") Save the children's responses. (See Writing/Oral Language section.)

ACTIVITIES

The [ ] around the text indicate a question.

Art

Have the children paint or draw Kitten and the firefly sitting under the full moon. Remind the children that the firefly is on the left-hand side of the page. Let the picture dry. Glue a circular trail of glitter to the firefly. Let this dry. Give the children two pipe cleaners, cutting them in half. Glue these to Kitten's face. Have the children listen to some facts about whiskers. Go to www.vetstreet/whiskers.com. Have them orally relay their favorite whisker facts to a friend.

Writing/Oral Language

- SAY: The firefly that is near Kitten is probably the one that got stuck on her tongue. We made conversation bubbles earlier, relaying what they might say to each other. Let's listen to a conversation between two children.

Ask two children to come up to the front of the room and have a conversation about a subject. (e.g., What they're going to do after school. Their favorite T.V. program. Their favorite game, etc.) Tell the children that a written conversation is called *dialogue*. Allow the children to choose a partner and have a conversation about a subject. When they're finished, ask them to relay some of the dialogue they had. Write it on a piece of paper. (e.g., Steve: "Will you be able to come over later?" John: "If I get the yard cleaned, I think my mom will let me go to your house," etc.)

- SAY: Now, we're going to create some dialogue between Kitten and Firefly. **[What do you think Kitten and Firefly might say to each other?]** Write a couple of statements on the board. (e.g., Kitten: "Why did you land on my tongue?" Firefly: "I wasn't watching where I was going." Kitten: "I was so surprised!" Firefly: "I'm so glad you didn't swallow me," etc.) Have the children think of additional dialogue that might occur between Kitten and Firefly and write this on a piece of paper. Have the children choose their favorite dialogue exchange and write it on a piece of paper. Ask them to read their dialogue exchange to a friend.

Science

- SAY: Whiskers are very important to a cat. Let's find out why they're important. Read the information on www.scienceforkids/whiskers.com, or www.vetstreet/whiskers.com, to relay some important facts to the children. Write some of these important facts on a piece of paper for the children to review. Have them write one sentence about a cat's whiskers and attach it to their drawing of Kitten, with the whiskers attached.

Math

- SAY: On a piece of paper, draw a picture of Kitten with two whiskers on each side of her face. Kitten has two whiskers on the right side of her face, and two whiskers on the left side of her face. **[Can anyone think of a way we could write a number sentence that would show the number of whiskers that Kitten has on her face?]**

Allow the children to respond, eventually determining that 2 + 2 = 4. They could write their own number sentence, drawing Kitten's whiskers under each number to represent the number sentence. (e.g., 2 whiskers + 2 whiskers = 4 whiskers.) or they could try different combinations of whiskers on Kitten's face to extend the lesson. (e.g., 3 + 3 = 6, 4 + 4 = 8, 5 + 5 = 10, etc.)

TEXT: So she pulled...

> **Direct the children's attention to the page where Kitten is jumping off the steps. Encourage them to answer the following questions in complete sentences.**

The [ ] around the text indicate a question.

- **[What do you see in the picture?]** (See Art section.)

- SAY: The author tells us that she "pulled herself together." Explain to the children that pulling yourself together means that you need to work or think through a problem you might be having. Give the children examples, such as: When you have a hard math problem to solve, you could just give up, or you could say to yourself, "I'll come back to this problem later." You pulled yourself together, making the decision to solve it. Here's another example: "I remember a time when I swung and had two strikes at a baseball game. I had to have a short conversation with myself. I didn't want to strike out, so I reminded myself that I was perfectly capable of hitting that ball! I pulled myself together."

Have the children discuss situations in which they pulled themselves together. Remind them that they won't always be able to solve or accomplish their goal, but they tried, and that is important. It shows that they have determination. (See Writing section below.) (below).

- SAY: The author tells us that Kitten "wiggled her bottom," before she jumped. **[Why did she "wiggle her bottom"?]**

- **[What do you think will happen after she jumps?]**

- SAY: The author tells us that Kitten "sprang" from the top step of the porch. **[Why do you think Kitten did that?]** (e.g., She wants to get the "bowl of milk" in the sky.)

- **[Do you think that's a good idea? Why or why not?]** (See Writing and Math sections.)

ACTIVITIES

The [ ] around the text indicate a question.

Art

Have the children illustrate this page, using a black color-wash. Have the children use a white crayon to draw Kitten and the moon on a piece of dark blue construction paper. Have them use a different color crayon, such as tan, to create the steps and the railing. Tell the children that they are to press the crayon thoroughly into the paper, leaving no open spaces. When they've finished the crayon drawing, have them cover the entire picture with a watery mixture of black paint. The watery black mixture will absorb into the construction paper, but it won't absorb into the crayon, leaving a vivid picture.

Writing

- Ask the children if they remember what the word *synonym* means. Synonyms are words that mean the same thing. Give them some examples. (e.g., Happy, glad, unhappy, sad, etc.) Show the children a thesaurus. Tell them they can find similar words in a thesaurus.

- SAY: The author told us that Kitten *sprang* from the porch. Let's find some words that mean the same thing. Look up the word *sprang* to find similar words. Write these words under the word *sprang*. (e.g., jump, leap, etc.) Have the children create a synonym flower. Start by writing the word *sprang* in the center of the flower, then write similar words around the individual petals.

Have the children write one sentence using the word *sprang*. Be available to help them sound out the words they use in their sentence. They could attach this sentence to the black color-wash illustration of Kitten.

- To follow up on their earlier discussion about "pulling themselves together," ask them to write a short paragraph about their experience. Be available to help them sound out words they'll use in their paragraph. Allow the children to read these experiences to the class, but don't force anyone to participate unless they choose to do so. Be sure to praise their courage, persistence, and determination in the face of a struggle.

Science

Have the children research how far different animals can jump. Search the internet by entering: How far can a tiger jump? The internet tells you about each individual animal. (e.g., tiger = 12 feet, kangaroo = 25 feet, gazelle = 30 feet, cheetah = 35 feet, lion = 36 feet, etc.) Make a class list. (e.g., cat, lion, cheetah, jaguar, etc.) Compare the distances that different animals can jump.

- Say Kitten had to use her muscles when she *sprang* from the top step. Show me some of your muscles. **[What is a muscle?]** Read the information on www.scienceforkids/muscles.com to learn more about them. Have the children look up muscles in an encyclopedia. Challenge the children to learn ten human muscles.

- After examining the various muscles in an encyclopedia or online, have the children draw and label some muscles. Challenge them to memorize ten additional muscles.

Math

- SAY: The author told us that Kitten *sprang* from the step. **[How could we determine how far she jumped?]** We could measure the distance. **[How do we measure things?]** List all the possible ways we could measure things. (e.g., We could use pencils, paper clips, our feet, our hands, our whole body, books, etc.) Talk about how we usually measure things, such as by using a ruler, yardstick, or meter stick. Hold up each measurement tool for the children to examine.

- SAY: Let's measure our room. Let's decide how we're going to measure it. Let the children vote on what measurement tool they'd like to use. Note: The first time they measure the room, let them choose a tool that isn't usually used, such as a pencil, their feet, a paper clip, etc. The second time they measure the room, have them use a standard measurement tool, such as a ruler or a yardstick. Have the children write down their measurements on an index card, to see if they have similar measurements. If the measurements aren't similar, discuss why they varied. (e.g., If they used a pencil, the length of the pencil might not have been the same for each student. If they used their feet, their feet might not be the same length.) Now, use a standard measurement tool, and have them record their measurements on another index card.

Record the results on a piece of paper. **[How did using the standard measurement tool vary from the first measurement tool?]** (e.g., It was more accurate.)

- Review the prior discussion about the word *sprang*. Discuss how the author tells us that Kitten *sprang* from the top step of the porch. (i.e., She jumped from the top step.) Before the children do this activity, have them write down on an index card how far they think they could jump. Remind them to write their name on the back of the card. Put these cards inside an envelope and compare them to their actual jump. Take the children outside and explain to them that they're going to jump from a starting line, like Kitten sprang from the porch. Create a starting line, where the children place their toes and touch this line. When they're ready, have them practice jumping as far as possible. They may want to try different methods before the actual measurement. For the "official" jump, an adult should record each child's jump, one child at a time. Allow each child two attempts, with the adult recording the longest jump. Take the children inside the classroom and record the results on a piece of paper. (See example below.) Allow each child to record their "x" on the paper, representing their individual jump. Have the adult who's recording the measurement round each measurement to the nearest half-foot.

			x	x	
	x	x	x	x	x
x	x	x	x	x	x
3 feet	**3 ½ feet**	**4 feet**	**4 ½ feet**	**5 feet**	**5 ½ feet**

Have the children cut strings representing their longest individual jump. From the envelope, take out the index cards on which they wrote down their predictions about how far they thought they could jump. Was their estimated jump longer or shorter than their actual jump? You can extend the lesson by asking the children to measure their "jumping strings" in different measurements. For example, **[How many inches, feet, or yards were you able to jump?]**

TEXT: But Kitten only...

Direct the children's attention to the page where Kitten has landed at the bottom of the steps. Encourage them to answer the following questions in complete sentences.

The [ ] around the text indicate a question.

- **[What do you see in the picture?]**

- **[Why do you think Kitten "tumbled"?]** (See Writing/Oral Language section.)

- **[What advice would you give Kitten?]** (See Writing/Oral Language section.)

- SAY: There is a saying that goes, "Cats always land on their feet." **[What do you think this means?] [Do you think it's true?]** (See Science section below.)

- SAY: Look carefully at the bottom of Kitten's paw. **[Does anyone know what we call this circular area?]** (e.g., Pads.)

- **[Why do you think pads are important?]** (e.g., The pads are important because Kitten walks on them. They must be tough enough to walk on sharp rocks, etc.)

- **[How do we protect our feet?]** (e.g., We wear shoes, which have tough leather on the bottom.)

ACTIVITIES

The [ ] around the text indicate a question.

Writing/Oral Language

- SAY: The author tells us that Kitten "tumbled." Let's try to name some synonyms that mean the same as tumbled. Write the children's responses on a piece of paper. Use a thesaurus to find similar words. (e.g., Fell, stumbled, toppled over, etc.) Have the children write one sentence with the word *tumbled*.

- **[What parts of Kitten's body did she hurt when she tumbled?]** (e.g., Well, it said she bumped her nose, ear, and tail.)

- **[Kitten tumbled off the steps and bumped her nose, ear, and tail. What do you think Kitten is thinking?]** (e.g., I'm not sure I'll try that again! That bowl of milk isn't easy to reach!)

After they've discussed Kitten tumbling off the steps, have the children pretend to be Advice Experts. Tell them that an Advice Expert is someone who gives advice to help people. **[If you could give Kitten one piece of advice, what would it be?]** Have the children write one sentence of advice to Kitten. (e.g., Kitten, STOP trying to chase that bowl of milk! It's really the moon, which is thousands of miles away!)

Science

The children discussed whether they thought cats always landed on their feet. Go to the internet and type: Does a cat always land on its feet? Read the information on a site you found. Relay some of the interesting information to the children.

- **[Does anyone know what the word *momentum* means?]**
  Go to www.scienceforkids/momentum.com and read the information to the children. There are some activities that they might enjoy doing.

Have the children conduct their own momentum experiments. Have different sizes/weights of balls moving toward various objects. (e.g., small plastic figurines, miniature plastic bowling pins, empty match boxes, etc.) Allow them to experiment with pushing the various balls with different amounts of force across a table. Talk about appropriate behavior during this investigation. (e.g., No throwing the balls, etc.) They might have to go outside to do this activity. **[What did you discover?]** Make a list of their observations on a piece of paper.

Math

- On a piece of paper, write *Yes* and *No*. Tell the children that they're going to predict whether Kitten will try to jump off the porch again. Have the children write *Yes* or *No* on a sticky note and place their sticky note on either the *Yes* or *No* space. Count the number of *Yes* and *No* votes and create a bar graph.

Have the children create a bar graph from the above question. Give the children a piece of 1-inch graph paper, allowing them to color in the number of *Yes* and *No* votes. Emphasize to the children that each 1-inch section represents one vote. Talk about how the bar graph should be labeled. For example, the question at the top of the bar graph could read: Will Kitten Jump Off the Porch Again? The *Yes* votes could be colored red, while the *No* votes could be colored blue. (Show examples of bar graphs for the children to see.)

TEXT: Still, there was...

> **Direct the children's attention to the page where Kitten is licking her paw. Encourage them to answer in complete sentences.**

The [ ] around the text indicate a question.

- **[What do you see in the picture?]**

- **[Why do you think Kitten is licking her paw?]** (e.g., Well, she fell off the steps and licking her paw might make it feel better, etc.)

- SAY: Look at Kitten's face. **[What do you think she's thinking now?]** (e.g., Maybe that "bowl of milk" is just too far away.)

- **[Do you think Kitten will make another attempt to get the "bowl of milk"?] [What do you think she'll do next?]** Write the children's predictions on a piece of paper. (See Writing section below.)

- SAY: Young kittens are able to do different things at different times. For example, a kitten is born with its eyes shut, however, it will open its eyes several days later. (See Science section below.)

Go to the internet and type: Kittens opening their eyes for the first time. You'll find some interesting information and videos to view.

- Invite a veterinarian to class to discuss the developmental stages of a young kitten's life. If this isn't possible, bring in books from the library that show their growth. Write this information on a sheet of paper. The children could make a timeline of the information they discovered.

ACTIVITIES

The [ ] around the text indicate a question.

Writing

The children predicted whether they thought Kitten would make another attempt to get the "bowl of milk." Have them write one sentence about what they think she might do in the future.

Science

Refer to the previous discussion/presentation of what young kittens are able to do at different times. Make a timeline together of the things they can do. (e.g., One month, two months, three months, four months, etc.)

TEXT: So she chased...

Direct the children's attention to the page where Kitten is walking in five different panels on the page. Encourage them to answer the following questions in complete sentences.

The [ ] around the text indicate a question.

- **[What do you see in the picture?]** (See Art section.)

- **[Where were some of the places she went when she tried chasing the "bowl of milk"?]** (e.g., The sidewalk, the garden, the field, the hills, and the pond.)

- **[What do you think Kitten is thinking at this point?]** Direct the children's attention to the final expression on Kitten's face.

- Point to the pictures of Kitten chasing the "bowl of milk" on the sidewalk, the garden, the field, the hills, and the pond. **[Do you think Kitten is getting closer to the "bowl of milk"?]**

- Look at the bottom picture frame. Have the children describe Kitten's expression. (e.g., Confused, tired, bewildered, etc.) Have the children model various expressions, such as confused, surprised, perplexed, etc.

- After the children have discussed Kitten's expression, review the descriptive words they used. Tell them that descriptive words are called *adjectives*. Adjectives describe things. Hold up a pencil and describe the qualities of the pencil. (e.g., It's long, thin, yellow, pointy, etc.) Tell the children that we used adjectives when we described Kitten's expression. We said she was confused, tired, bewildered, etc. We described her expression with adjectives.

- As a follow-up to the previous discussion, have the children draw and describe a friend, using adjectives. (e.g., Tom is tall, he has blonde hair, he has blue eyes, he is friendly, he is smart, etc.)

- **[What would Kitten have to do to reach the "bowl of milk"?]** (e.g., Kitten would need to go to space to reach the moon, which would require a rocket. She would need special equipment, etc.) (See Art section.)

ACTIVITIES

The [ ] around the text indicate a question.

Art

- Review the five panels that the illustrator used on this page to show where Kitten was heading. Have the children draw and color other locations where Kitten might go. (e.g., On a wall, on a roof, in a tree, in a vacant lot, etc.)

- SAY: Earlier, we discussed how we'd get Kitten to the "bowl of milk." She'd need to take a rocket into space. Today, we'll create our own rocket for Kitten.

Have the children bring in toilet paper tubes and paint them a bright color. Let them dry. Decorate the toilet paper tubes with stars, glitter, or stickers. Cut around the round circle on the Resource page (e.g., Rocket top.) and let the children paint and decorate it. Let this dry. Cut from the dot in the center of the circle to the outside of the circular edge on the line. Turn the circular cone until it fits the top of the toilet paper tube. Glue the overlapping edge to form the top of the rocket. Let this dry. Glue the top of the rocket to the toilet paper tube, completing the rocket. (See Resource section.)

- SAY: Kitten's family is probably worried that she won't return home. **[What are some ways we could find Kitten?]** Discuss some possible ways that Kitten could be found. (e.g., The family could walk around the neighborhood looking for her. They could ask their friends to help in the search, etc.) Relay to the children that people with lost pets often make posters for their neighbors to see. Tell them that they're going to create a Wanted Poster for Kitten. **[What things would be important on our poster?]** Make a list of the things the children say are important to include. Write the following on a piece of paper. Draw a quick picture of Kitten on the paper.

WANTED POSTER

Writing/Oral Language

- Make a map of Kitten's adventures. On a piece of butcher paper, make a sample map for the children to see. Quickly draw the five different locations on the butcher paper. (e.g., The sidewalk, garden, field, hills, and pond.) Give the children a large sheet of butcher paper. Talk about a compass rose, relaying that the top of their paper will be North, the bottom of the paper will be South, the right side of the paper will be East, and the left side of the paper will be West. Have the children decide where they'll draw the various panels. They could put streets next to the panels, making it easier to direct Kitten's movements. The children can decide where they want the search to begin by writing "START SEARCH" at some location on their paper. The children could orally relay directions to a friend, having them move a small car or a plastic Kitten in that direction. Before the children do this activity on their own, the teacher could have them practice getting to a location by coming up to the front of the room and directing a student how to proceed on the sample map. Invite one child at a time to come up and either give or follow the directions. (e.g., Place your car on the "START SEARCH" location. Have your car move north on First Street. When you reach Pine Street, head east. Continue east until you reach Fifth Street. Head south on Fifth Street, etc.) The children should end up at the pond.

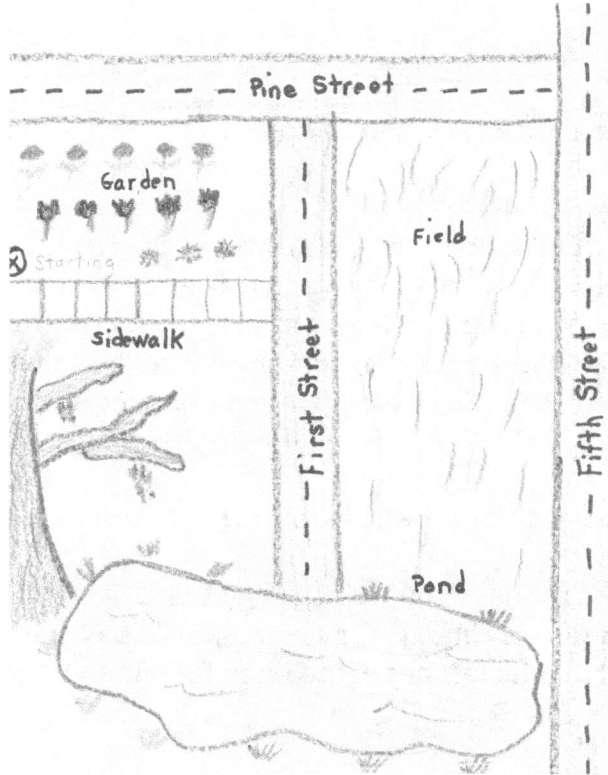

Science

- Throw a ball into the air and ask the following questions: **[Why do things fall down when you throw them up into the air?]** Allow the children to respond. Read the information on www.scienceforkids/gravity.com. Also try www.gravityforkids.com. They'll enjoy the information presented on these sites. Drop two different items, each weighing a different amount. Have the children observe what happened to these two items. **[Did one item fall to the ground first?] [Did they fall to the ground at the same time?] [Why do you think this happened?]**

Have the children make a list of directional words. SAY: We know that items thrown **_up_** will eventually come **_down_**. **[What are some other directional words?]** Make a list of every directional word they can think of. (e.g., up, down, over, under, behind, etc.)

TEXT: Still, there was...

> **Direct the children's attention to the page where Kitten is crouched down with her left paw raised. Encourage them to answer the following questions in complete sentences.**

The [ ] around the text indicate a question.

- **[What do you see in the picture?]**

- **[What do you think Kitten is going to do?]**

> **Direct the children's attention to how Kitten is crouched down, with her left paw raised. [Do you think Kitten is thinking about making another jump?] Have several of the children come to the front of the room and practice crouching like Kitten. Let another group come to the front of the room and do the same thing. Allow each child an opportunity to crouch, lifting their left hand toward the moon.** (See Science section below.)

- **[Do you remember which paw Kitten raised?]** (e.g., Her left paw.)

- During her walk, Kitten has been trying to get the "bowl of milk." **[Would the milk spoil in a short period of time?]** (e.g., It probably wouldn't spoil in a short period of time.) **[What would happen to a bowl of milk left out in the open for a long period of time?]** (e.g., It probably would spoil.) (See Science section below.)

- SAY: Kitten certainly loves milk! **[Can you name some things that are made with milk?]** List some milk products on a piece of paper. (e.g., Milk shakes, ice cream, cottage cheese, custard, cheese, butter, etc.) Ask the children to write down on a sticky note their favorite food made with milk. Have them put their sticky note under that food, counting the total number of responses.

- SAY: Baby kittens drink milk from the mother because it's the food that's naturally produced by her to feed her kittens. You eat and drink things that help you grow, such as milk. Milk is a drink that is enjoyed by many people, because it has many nutrients. A nutrient is something in the milk that is healthy for your body.

Have the children examine a milk carton, listing the percentages of fat, cholesterol, sodium, carbohydrates, and proteins.

- To extend this discussion, have a variety of empty boxes, cans, and containers for the children to examine. Tell them that high percentages of sugar and salt aren't necessarily healthy for the body. Encourage them to examine various cans and labels at home. Tell them that healthy food choices should include fruits, vegetables, grains, and proteins.

- As a culminating event for the milk products discussion, have the children make butter. (See Science section below.)

ACTIVITIES

The [ ] around the text indicate a question.

Science

- After the previous discussion about what would happen to a bowl of milk left out in the open, bring in a pint of milk and pour it into a clear, flat container. Have the children observe and record what they see and smell for several days. You could do this as a class, and have the children record their observations independently. Write the following on a piece of paper: How Does the Milk Look and Smell?

Day One	Day Two	Day Three	Day Four
It smells fine.	It doesn't have a smell.	It's beginning to smell.	It stinks!
(Drawing)	(Drawing)	(Drawing)	(Drawing)

- As a culminating event for the milk products discussion, have the children make butter. Have them sit in a circle. Show a carton of heavy cream and tell them that the heavy cream separates from the raw milk, with the heavy cream sitting on the top of the milk. This heavy cream is scooped off the top of the raw milk to make ice cream, butter, and other foods that require heavy cream. Place the heavy cream into two or three clear, plastic containers. Make sure the lids are completely sealed. Place the three containers in different locations around the circle, so that the children will have several opportunities to shake the containers. Tell the children that shaking the containers will make the heavy cream separate. You might want to play some music while they're shaking the containers, stopping the music when it's time to pass the containers. Emphasize that they are to pass the containers in the same direction each time. (e.g., Pass the containers to your left.) Have the children shake the containers until the butter forms. When the butter is ready, pour off the liquid and spread the butter onto some crackers. Enjoy!

Math

- SAY: Kitten was so eager to get that "bowl of milk" in the sky, that she went to several locations to get it. It's too bad she didn't know that her family had a lot of milk waiting for her at home.

Show the children various milk containers, such as a pint, quart, half-gallon, and gallon container. Tell the children that each container holds a different amount of liquid. Hold up a measuring cup and demonstrate that two cups of water would fill the pint container. Hold up the pint container and demonstrate that two pints of water would fill the quart container, etc. Have a measurement center set up within the classroom, where the children can experiment with the different containers. Talk about appropriate behavior at the center. They are to carefully measure the liquid, being careful not to spill the contents. This experiment could be done with one or two children at a time, with the teacher supervising the experience.

- As a homework project, have the children compare the prices of different brands of milk in different sized containers. (e.g., The pint size of brand A = $, the pint size of brand B = $, etc.) Make a class list of what they discovered.

- After the children have made a class list of the sizes, brands, and costs of the different products, determine which brand they thought was the best value. (e.g., You could divide the cost of the milk by the number of ounces.) Discuss good shopping techniques.

- **[Is it always good to buy a product with the lowest price? Why or why not?]**

- They could determine how many glasses of milk they'd personally drink in a week. (e.g. I drink three glasses of milk each day. There are seven days in a week, so I would drink twenty-one glasses of milk in a week.) Have the children draw seven circles on a piece of paper. Have them draw three dots in the center of each circle. Count the dots together. The children should discover that twenty-one dots are inside the circles. This represents the number of glasses of milk they would drink in a week.

TEXT: So she ran...

Direct the children's attention to the page where Kitten is climbing up the tree. Encourage them to answer the following questions in complete sentences.

The [ ] around the text indicate a question.

- **[What do you see in the picture?]**

- **[Would you say Kitten was persistent in trying to reach the "bowl of milk"? Why or why not?]** (e.g., The text said that Kitten "climbed and climbed and climbed," so she must have been persistent in her attempts.)

- **[How is Kitten attempting to reach the "bowl of milk" this time?]**

- **[Is Kitten getting closer to the "bowl of milk"? Why or why not?]**

- SAY: Kitten is trying to climb to the top of a tall tree. **[How tall can trees grow?]** Read the information on www.scienceforkids/talltrees.com. It has some interesting information that the children will enjoy. Help the children research the height of different trees. (e.g., Coast Redwood, Giant Sequoia, Coast Douglas Fir, Sitka Spruce, and Australian Mountain Ash.) (e.g., The redwood tree can grow to approximately 370 feet.) Make a list of the different heights of various trees.

- **[Why is Kitten able to cling to the tree?]** (e.g., She's using her sharp claws to cling to the tree.) (See Math section below.)

- **[Which animals have claws?]** Make a list of these animals. (e.g., Cats, lions, tigers, bobcats, etc.)

ACTIVITIES

The [ ] around the text indicate a question.

Science

- Go to a lumber store and get a cross section of a tree, or go online to www.scienceforkids/treerings.com to show a cross section of a tree. The children will enjoy hearing the information presented on this site. If you're able to obtain a cross section of a tree, allow the children to examine, feel, smell, and count the rings on this cross section. Explain to the children that each ring represents a period of growth for the tree. Some rings are wider than others because there was more growth. Some rings are closer together because there was less growth.

Have the children draw a cross section of a tree. It can be a cross section from a sample, or an example they've seen on the website listed previously.

Have the children name as many trees as they can. Make a list of the trees that the children know, adding additional trees as they discover new ones. (e.g., Pine, spruce, alder, redwood, oak, etc.)

Have the children draw the various parts of a tree. Demonstrate by drawing and relaying each part of the tree on a piece of paper. (e.g., Here are the roots of the tree, here is the trunk of the tree, here are the branches of the tree, etc.) Have lots of books available for the children to examine.

- Explain to the children that trees are good for our environment because they produce oxygen. Explain that oxygen is what we breathe to live. Invite a representative from a local nursery to come to class to discuss the importance of trees. Many businesses are willing to relay this information to children.

- Call a local nursery or a nationwide store to see if they'd donate a small tree. Many organizations are willing to donate items for educational purposes. Ask the administration if there's a special location where the tree could be planted, enabling it to be watered along with other plants.

Math

- **[If Kitten moved three inches with each step up the tree, how many steps would it take to reach the top of an eight-foot tree?]** On a piece of paper, draw a large tree. Tell the children that 3 inches + 3 inches + 3 inches + 3 inches =12 inches, or one foot. Hold up a ruler and explain to the children that a ruler would show 12 inches, or one foot. Draw eight sections (8 feet) on the tree. Tell the children that this represents an eight-foot tree. Tell them that if Kitten wanted to reach the top of an eight-foot tree, she'd have to take thirty-two steps until she reached the top of the tree. Take the children outside and have them move thirty-two steps in one direction. Tell the children that their steps would be longer than Kitten's steps, but it would take thirty-two steps for her to reach the top of the tree. They can practice counting as they take their steps. You could have them hop, jump, or dance these steps.

- To extend this lesson, you can demonstrate the height of an eight-foot tree. Have the children cut out several three-inch strips of paper, representing the three inches Kitten would move with each step. (e.g., If you have twenty children in class, you'd need to have each child cut out two three-inch pieces of paper to measure the height of an eight-foot tree. This would show the thirty-two steps that Kitten would need to take to reach the top of the tree. If you have fewer children, they'd need to cut out more three-inch strips of paper.) Take the children outside and place thirty-two strips of paper onto a flat surface. The strips of paper should be taped one after the other, equaling the height of an eight-foot tree. Allow the children to lie down next to the strips of paper so they can visually see how their height compares to an eight-foot tree. You might need to find an indoor space to do this project, as the wind could interfere with this project. Take the long strips of taped paper inside the classroom and place them in a location where the children can see it. Make sure you have enough tape on the strips of paper to hold it firmly together.

TEXT: But Kitten still...

> **Direct the children's attention to the page where Kitten is sitting at the top of the tree. Encourage them to answer the following questions in complete sentences.**

The [ ] around the text indicate a question.

- **[What do you see in the picture?]** (See Art section.)

- SAY: Look carefully at Kitten's face. **[How would you describe her expression?]** Make a list of possible words on a piece of paper. (e.g., She looks frustrated, tired, unhappy, confused, etc.)

- SAY: The author tells us that Kitten was "scared." **[What do you think Kitten should do to solve her problem?]** Make a list of possible solutions. (e.g., She should not go out at night! She should stay home at night and enjoy her family.)

- **[Have you ever felt scared like Kitten?]** (See Writing section below.)

- **[How do you think Kitten could let someone know she was in trouble?]** (e.g., She'd probably start howling!) Take the children outside and let them demonstrate how Kitten might howl at the top of the tree.

- **[Do you know how animals make howling sounds?]** (See Science section below.)

- **[Have you ever felt frustrated like Kitten, because you couldn't get something you really wanted?]** (See Writing section below.)

ACTIVITIES

The [ ] around the text indicate a question.

Art

Have the children illustrate this page, drawing or painting Kitten's perplexed expression. Let this dry. Have the children cut out leaves from different colors of tissue paper and glue them to the tree.

Writing

- SAY: The author tells us that Kitten was "scared." **[Have you ever been really scared?]** Ask some of the children to share a time when they were scared. Write their responses on a piece of paper. (e.g., I was scared when my mother had to visit my aunt for two days. I was scared when my brother hurt his arm, etc.) They could copy one sentence from the paper or create a sentence of their own. Be available to help them sound out the words.

CALDECOTT ACTIVITY BOOK

- SAY: The author tells us that Kitten couldn't reach the little "bowl of milk." She looks tired, frustrated, and disappointed. **[Have you ever felt like that?]** On a piece of paper, write how the children felt when they couldn't get something they really wanted. They could copy one sentence from the paper or create a sentence of their own. Be available to help them sound out the words.

Science

- SAY: Kitten might have started howling when she got to the top of the tree. The author tells us she was "scared."

Read the information on www.scienceforkids/howlingsounds.com. There is some interesting information that the children will enjoy hearing. Have the children place their hand over their throat and hum. They will feel a vibration. This vibration is caused by their vocal cords moving. Go to www.scienceforkids/vocalcords.com and read the information listed there. There's another site called "Making Vocal Cords," which shows how to demonstrate the movement of their vocal cords. It's very simple and it could be done in the Science Center.

Have the children draw and label the vocal cords. Have books available for them to examine and read. An encyclopedia would also have important information.

TEXT: Then, in the...

> **Direct the children's attention to the page where Kitten is sitting at the top of the tree looking down into the pond. Encourage them to answer the following questions in complete sentences.**

The [ ] around the text indicate a question.

- **[What do you see in the picture?]** (See Art section.)

- SAY: The author tells us that Kitten sees "another bowl of milk." **[What "bowl of milk" does she see?]** (e.g., She thinks the round circle in the pond is a bigger bowl of milk.)

- **[What does the author tell us about this "bowl of milk" compared to the last one she thought she saw?]** (e.g., She thinks this bowl of milk is bigger.)

- **[Why does this "bowl of milk" appear bigger?]** (See Science section below.)

- **[Do you think the "bowl of milk" looks bigger because the moon is shining down on the pond? Why or why not?]**

- **[What are some ways that we can make things bigger?]** (See Science section below.)

- SAY: Look carefully at the tree. **[Why do you think the tree has so few leaves?]** (e.g., Well, it might be fall, when the leaves are dropping off the tree.)

- **[What do you think Kitten will do now?]** Make a list of things you think Kitten will do. (e.g., I think she's going to jump into the "bowl of milk.")

- SAY: The author writes, "What a night!" **[Why do you think it was an important night?]** On a piece of paper, write why the children think it was an important night. (See Writing section below.)

- **[Have you ever had an important night?]** On a piece of paper, write some of the children's responses. (e.g., It was an important night when I lost my tooth. It was an important night when my sister was born. It was an important night when my dad came home from the military, etc.) (See Writing section below.)

- **[Do you think it's dangerous for Kitten to be climbing the tree at night? Why or why not?]**

- SAY: Cats are supposed to have good eyesight at night. **[Do you think your eyesight is as good as Kitten's?]** (See Science section below.)

- **[Did you know that light can travel?]** It can travel very, very fast.

- SAY: Let's clap our hands. Clapping our hands took about a second. In that time, light was able to travel 186,000 miles. A car can't travel that fast. A plane can't travel that fast. If you shine a flashlight at night, you can see the light from a long distance away. **[Does anyone know what the word reflection means?]** It means that light bounces off things. If you look in a mirror, your face is reflected in the mirror. (See Science section below.)

- SAY: Look carefully at this picture. You can see the moon reflected in the pond. The light coming from the moon bounces off the water in the pond to reflect the shape of the moon. So, it looks like the moon is in the water.

ACTIVITIES

The [ ] around the text indicate a question.

Art

Have the children illustrate this page using a collage technique. Have them cut out the tree, leaves, hills, pond, bushes, and moon, using different colors of construction and tissue paper. Glue these onto a piece of dark blue construction paper. They can add layers of paper to create a collage. When they've finished their picture, cover the entire picture with a watery glue mixture to hold the layers of paper in place.

Writing

- The author writes, "What a night!" Review the reasons why the children think it's a special night and have them copy one sentence from their earlier discussion. If they'd prefer, they can write their own reasons why it's an important night. Be available to sound out the words for them.

- Review the paper that describes when the children had an important night. (e.g., When I was five, my mother gave birth to my sister. It was a very important night. My mother had a suitcase packed with new clothes for the baby. I could hardly wait for her to come home ...) They can copy a sentence from the paper or write their own sentence. Be available to sound out the words.

Science

- SAY: We can make things look bigger by using a magnifying glass.

Read the information on www.scienceforkids/magnification.com. There is some interesting information for the children to enjoy. Have a magnifying glass set up in the Science Center, with various items for the children to examine. (e.g., Rocks, leaves, grass, sand, flowers, small pictures, paper clips, etc.)

- Read the information about reflection of light on www.scienceforkids/reflection.com. Have mirrors available for them to see their reflection.

- As a follow-up project to the reflection information, have the children make a mirror. (See Resource section.) Draw and cut out the mirror and circle in the Resource section. To make the mirror stronger, trace around the mirror and the circle on a piece of poster board. Allow the children to paint and decorate the mirror. Cover the circle with a piece of aluminum foil and press it to the backside of the circle. Glue the backside portion of the aluminum foil to the front of the mirror. Optional: Glue the entire mirror onto another piece of poster board and have the children write one sentence about reflection of light. Encourage them to tell their family what they learned.

- Review the information on www.scienceforkids/reflection.com. Demonstrate how a mirror reflects light. Bounce a ball against a wall. **[What did the ball do?]** (e.g., It bounced back.) Tell the children that light is like the bouncing ball—it bounces off objects and comes back to us. Have the children print their name on a piece of paper. Have them hold up their printed name to a mirror. What did they discover? Now, have them hold up the mirror and try printing their name. What did they discover?

- Read the information about the night vision of cats. Go to the internet and type: How do cats see at night? Have the children orally relay one fact to a friend.

- Read the information about the human eye on www.scienceforkids/humaneye.com. Have the children orally relay one fact to a friend.

- Show the children a picture of the human eye. Have them sit with a partner and look at their eyes. Have one child close his/her eyes for two to three minutes and then have their partner watch what happens when they open their eyes. (e.g., The pupil dilates, or gets smaller.) Tell the children that if they don't keep their eyes closed for the entire time, the experiment won't work. Let the partner do the same thing. Have books available for the children to read.

TEXT: So she raced...

Direct the children's attention to the page where Kitten is climbing down the tree. Encourage them to answer the following questions in complete sentences.

The [ ] around the text indicate a question.

- **[What do you see in the pictures?]**

- **[Why do you think Kitten decided to climb down from the top of the tree?]** (e.g., She saw a bigger "bowl of milk" from the top of the tree and she wants to get it, etc.)

- SAY: Make a prediction of what you think is going to happen to Kitten. (e.g., I think Kitten will run to the "bowl of milk," but she'll get wet!)

- SAY: Kitten is using muscles to go down the tree. Show me some of your muscles. (See Science section below.)

- Do you know that a cat can jump about seven times its height? **[Do you think you could jump seven times your height?]** Ask one of the children to come to the front of the room and measure their height. If they measured four feet tall, that means they would be able to jump twenty-eight feet. (See Science section below.)

- SAY: The author said that Kitten "raced through the grass." **[How fast do you think a cat can run?]** List the children's predictions on a piece of paper. Write their name next to their prediction. (See Science section below.)

- SAY: On the next page, the author describes Kitten's actions by saying, she "leaped with all her might." The word *leap* is a verb. A verb is a word that shows action. (See Writing section below.)

- **[Do you think cats like water?]** Most cats aren't especially fond of water. **[Why do you think Kitten was willing to jump into the pond?]** (e.g., She wants that "bowl of milk" so much, that's she's willing to chase after it.)

- **[Do you think Kitten knows that she's going to land in the water?]** (e.g., She probably doesn't realize that the "bowl of milk" is a cold, wet pond. It's the reflection of the moon.)

- **[Do you think Kitten will be surprised when she ends up in the water?]** (e.g., I think she'll be very surprised!)

- **[Has there been a time when you did something you weren't especially fond of doing?]** On a piece of paper, make a class list of the children's responses. (e.g., I jumped into the pool from the high platform. I fed an animal at the petting zoo. I ate a new vegetable, etc.) (See Writing section below.)

- **[Even though you didn't want to do it, why did you think it was worthwhile?]** (e.g., I wanted to overcome my fear of heights. I thought it would be fun to feed an animal. I thought it would be healthy to eat a new vegetable, etc.)

- **[What do you think Kitten will say when she discovers that the "bowl of milk" is a big pond, filled with water?]** (See Writing section below.)

ACTIVITIES

The [ ] around the text indicate a question.

Art

Have the children illustrate the panels on these pages. When they've completed their illustrations, have them write a short sentence for each panel. (e.g., Kitten jumps down from the tree. Kitten runs toward the "bowl of milk." Kitten is near the edge of the pond. Kitten jumps, etc.)

Writing

- SAY: We learned earlier that the word *leap* is a verb. A verb shows action.

Invite a child to the front of the room to demonstrate an action. Allow each child to come up and show one action. (e.g., Waving, dancing, blinking, moving a finger, etc.) Ask them what other verbs could be used instead of the word *leap*. Look in a thesaurus to find other words that mean the same as *leap*. Make a list of these words on a piece of paper and have the children write one sentence with a verb. (e.g., Jumped, sprang, scurried, etc.)

- SAY: Earlier we discussed how we've done things that we weren't especially fond of doing. Kitten was willing to jump into the pond to get the "bowl of milk."

Review the class list they created earlier. Have the children copy or write one sentence about a time they did something they weren't especially fond of doing. (e.g., I thought it would be healthy to eat a new vegetable, etc.)

- SAY: Create conversation bubbles expressing what you think Kitten might say when she discovers that the "bowl of milk" is a cold, wet pond. (See Resource section.)
  (e.g., "Rats! How could I have known that the 'bowl of milk' would turn out to be a pond full of water? What was I thinking? That water was cold. I thought I'd have a big bowl of milk to enjoy!")

Science

- Earlier, the children showed some of their muscles. Tell them that it takes seventeen muscles in their face to form a smile and forty-three muscles to form a frown. Tell them that cats have muscles in their body, just like we do. Go to the internet and type: Diagram of cat muscles. This will show a detailed diagram. Note: There are websites that show skinned cats, so be careful when choosing a website. An encyclopedia will also have a picture of the various muscles in a cat's body. Tell the children the names of the leg muscles. Challenge them to learn an additional five to ten muscles.

Have the children draw and label some of the cat's muscles.

- After discussing how cats have the ability to jump seven times its height, show the children a ruler. Tell the children that a ruler measures one foot. If a cat measured one foot long, it would be able to jump seven feet. Allow the children to measure seven feet on a piece of butcher paper.

- Look at the children's predictions about how fast a cat can run. Go to the internet and type: How fast can a cat run? Read the information to the children. Tell them a cat can run at a top speed of about thirty miles per hour. Whose prediction came the closest? Explain to them that a car traveling on a city street usually travels about thirty miles per hour. If possible, give the winner of the prediction some cat stickers.

TEXT: Poor Kitten...

Direct the children's attention to the page where Kitten is in the pond. Encourage them to answer the following questions in complete sentences.

The [ ] around the text indicate a question.

- **[What do you see in the picture?]**

- **[How would you describe Kitten's expression?]** Write the children's responses on a piece of paper. (e.g., She looks amazed! She looks surprised. She looks upset, etc.)

- **[What advice would you give Kitten at this point?]** Write some of the children's responses on a piece of paper. (See Writing section below.)

- SAY: The author said that Kitten was "sad." **[Why do you think Kitten was sad?]** Write the children's responses on a piece of paper. (e.g., I think she was sad because she was fooled again! I think she was sad because she really thought she was going to have a lot of milk, etc.)

- **[How do you feel when you're sad?]** Write the children's responses on a piece of paper. (e.g., I feel yucky! I feel like I don't want to smile at anyone. I feel like I want to be left alone, etc.)

- **[Do you think animals have some of the same feelings as people? Why or why not?]**

- **[Do you think animals show signs of sadness or upset?]** Make a list of these signs on a piece of paper. (e.g., My cat twitches her tail when she's upset. My dog flattens his ears when something bothers him.

My dog growls in a low voice when she's upset, etc.) The author said that Kitten was "tired." **[Why do you think Kitten was tired?]** (e.g., She's tried several times to get the "bowl of milk," and failed.)

- **[Do you think cats need a lot of rest? Why or why not?]** (See Science section below.)

- SAY: People need rest too. **[How many hours of sleep do you get?]**

Ask one child to tell you when they go to bed and when they get up in the morning. Together, determine how many hours of sleep they get. If you have a large clock available, demonstrate the times on the clock. (e.g., I go to bed at 8:00 p.m. at night, and I get up around 7:00 a.m. in the morning. Show the movement of the clock's hands.) (e.g., We can count from 8:00 p.m. until 12:00 o'clock (midnight). That's four hours. From 12:00 a.m. to 7:00 a.m., that's another seven hours. So, 4 + 7 = 11. That's eleven hours of sleep each night.) (See Math section below.)

- SAY: The author said that Kitten was "hungry." She's been trying to reach the big bowl of milk for a long time. **[Do you think she'll give up searching for it? Why or why not?]**

- **[What are some good things for cats/kittens to eat?]** Make a list of their responses on a piece of paper. Ask some of the children who have a cat at home to share what they feed their cat.

- Ask the children to name several brands of cat food. Make a list of these products on a piece of paper. Ask the children to bring some product labels for different cat foods. Glue these to a piece of paper, so the children can examine the labels. Show them the ingredients list for several brands. **[Do you think different brands have the same ingredients? Why or why not? Why do you think that different brands of cat food have different ingredients?]**

- **[Do you know how much a bag or can of cat food costs?]** Have the children make predictions on a piece of paper. (See Math section below.)

- SAY: Kitten probably has plenty of food at home, but she had her mind made up to get that "bowl of milk." Her determination led her straight to the pond. **[What do you think about this?]**

- SAY: We know that Kitten was very determined to get the "bowl of milk." **[What do her actions tell you?]** Have the children use words that describe Kitten's attempts. (e.g., She was dedicated. She was determined. She was single-minded. She was focused. She had a purpose, etc.)

Have the children look in a thesaurus to make a list of words that describe Kitten's actions.

- **[What do you think Kitten's owners would say about her actions?]**

- **[Do you think Kitten's owners are worried about her?] [Do they know where she is?]**

ACTIVITIES

The [ ] around the text indicate a question.

Art

Have the children illustrate this page, trying to draw or paint Kitten's expression.

Writing

- SAY: The author said that Kitten was "sad."

Have the children brainstorm different times in their life when they've been sad. Write their responses on a piece of paper. (e.g., I was sad when I fell off my bike and bruised my arm. I was sad when my friend didn't call me, etc.) Have the children write a few sentences about a time when they were sad. The children can copy one of the sentences or create their own sentence. Be available to help them sound out the words.

- Review the children's responses about the advice they'd offer Kitten. (e.g., Kitten, your family has plenty of milk for you to drink at home. Stop trying to find that big bowl of milk, etc.) Have the children write some suggestions for Kitten. (e.g., Kitten, I suggest that you stay in your cozy house at night! Kitten, I suggest that you be happy with the milk your owners give you, etc.) They can copy one of the group suggestions or create their own sentence. Be available to help them sound out the words.

Science

- SAY: We discussed whether cats need a lot of rest. Go to the internet and type: Tell me about cats sleeping. Cats sleep about thirteen to fourteen hours a day! That's a long time to sleep. You probably sleep eight to ten hours a night, so cats sleep three to four hours longer than you do.

Math

- SAY: We discovered that cats need about thirteen to fourteen hours of sleep.

Have the children practice moving the hands on a clock to demonstrate various times. If you don't have a large clock, the children can easily make one. (See Resource section.) Cut out an eight-inch circle on a piece of poster board. Cut out the smaller circle in the Resource section with the numbers on the face of the clock. Glue the smaller circle to the eight-inch circle. Let this dry. Make two "hands," by cutting out two pointed pieces of poster board. One piece of poster board should be longer than the other, representing the minute hand. Use a hole punch to make holes at the ends of the minute and hour hand. Punch a hole in the center of their clock. A sharp pencil or pen should be used. Overlap the two "hands" and put an inch brad through them.

Put the "hands" through the center of the clock and make sure that it moves freely. Fold the brad on the back of the clock. When the children have completed their clock, give them different times to demonstrate. (e.g., Kitten goes to sleep at 8:00 a.m.) **[If she sleeps three hours in the morning, what time would it be?] That's right, it would be 11:00 a.m. [If you go to bed at 8:00 p.m. and get up at 6:00 a.m., how long did you sleep?]**

- Bring in grocery ads that show various cat food products. Talk about why different brands cost more. (e.g., The ingredients in some brands cost more than others. For example, real chicken pieces would be more expensive than soybean products.) You can show a soybean, so they know what it is. On a piece of paper, write down the names of three to five different cat food products. (e.g., Brand A, Brand B, Brand C, etc.) The cans or bags should be the same weight. List the price of each product under its name. Have the children compare the different prices. Together, determine how much money could be saved for a week by purchasing one brand of cat food versus another brand. They would first need to determine how much food Kitten would eat in a day. (e.g., One can in the morning and one can in the evening.)

- Bring in magazines and grocery ads. Have the children cut out every cat food product they can find from these sources. Have them glue the pictures to a piece of paper, creating a class collage.

TEXT: So she went...

> **Direct the children's attention to the page where Kitten got out of the pond. Encourage them to answer the following questions in complete sentences.**

The [ ] around the text indicate a question.

- **[What do you see in the pictures?]** (See Art section.)

- **[What do you think Kitten is thinking and feeling at this point in the story?] [Do you think she's learned anything from her experiences?]** Write the children's responses on a piece of paper. (See Writing section below.)

- **[Do you think it was a wise decision for Kitten to go home? Why or why not?]**

- **[Where will she have to go in order to get home?]** (e.g., She will have to go past the pond, the field, the garden, and walk down the sidewalk to get home.)

- **[When Kitten's owners see her, how do you think they'll react?] [Do you think they even know that she was gone?]**

- **[How long do you think Kitten was gone?]**

- **[Do you think Kitten might have encountered some hazards on her way home?]** Make a list of possible hazards on a piece of paper. (e.g., Kitten had to walk through a field, which had stickers and bugs. She was all alone at night, and she may have had to walk past other animals, etc.)

Have the children look carefully at the panel where water is dripping off of Kitten. **[Why doesn't the water simply *absorb*, or go into her fur?]** Make a list of the children's responses on a piece of paper. (See Science section below.)

- Talk about the repelling nature of fur and feathers. Bring in a large feather and demonstrate how water simply rolls off a feather when a few drops of water are placed on it. Use an eyedropper to drop the water onto the feather. Be sure to tilt the feather, so that the weight of the water doesn't separate the feathers. Allow the children to experiment with different pieces of fur, feathers, and pieces of fabric. Set these materials in the Science Center where the children can explore this principle. Talk about appropriate behavior in the Science Center.

- Read the information on www.scienceforkids/beavers.com. It gives some interesting facts about beavers. Beaver fur is designed to repel water. Have the children read and listen to the information about beaver fur. (See Science section below.)

- **[Do you think Kitten has learned anything from her explorations?]** Make a list of what they think she's learned. (See Writing section below.)

ACTIVITIES

The [ ] around the text indicate a question.

Art

Have the children work in groups, illustrating the various panels on these pages. Tell them that each panel must be illustrated, so they must decide as a group who will illustrate each panel. This allows them an opportunity to plan ahead, make decisions, and cooperate within a group to accomplish a task. When the children have drawn each panel, have them glue their illustrations onto a piece of poster board. Display each group's illustrations.

Writing

- SAY: We talked about what Kitten might have learned from her experiences.

Have the children review their comments and write one of the sentences or create their own sentence. (e.g., I've learned that the light from the moon makes the water look like a big bowl of milk. I've learned that I get tired when I'm searching for that milk! I've learned that the pond is very cold at night, etc.) Be available to help them sound out the words.

Science

- SAY: The picture of Kitten shows water dripping off her whiskers and fur. We talked earlier about why the water didn't absorb into her fur. **[Does anyone know what the word *repel* means?]** (i.e., It means to push back. The fur or feathers "push back" against the water.) Demonstrate the repelling action of a feather. Bring in a large feather and drip water over it, using an eyedropper. Tilt the feather, so that it allows the water to roll off the surface. Allow the children to experiment with different pieces of fur, feathers, or fabric. Set these materials in the Science Center, where the children can explore this principle.

- SAY: Beavers have fur that is designed to repel water. The word *repel* means that it pushes the water away.

Go to the internet and type in: Why does beaver fur repel water? Read the information on this website. It has some very interesting information that the children will enjoy hearing. You could also go to www.scienceforkids/beavers.com to learn more interesting facts about beavers.

TEXT: and there was...

> **Direct the children's attention to the page where there's a big bowl of milk on the porch. Encourage them to answer the following questions in complete sentences.**

The [ ] around the text indicate a question.

- **[What do you see in the picture?]**

- **[How do you think Kitten feels now?]** Make a list of the children's responses. (e.g., I think she's happy because she has a smile on her face. I think she's relieved to be home because she doesn't have to be wet, tired, or hungry. I think she's learned her lesson!) (See Writing section below.)

- **[Why do you think the family put the bowl of milk on the porch?]**

- **[Do you think Kitten will be able to drink the entire bowl of milk?]** (See Science section below.)

- SAY: Milk is a product that many animals and people enjoy.

Have the children examine the various milk labels to determine the fat content. (e.g., Nonfat milk, 2% milk, whole milk, cream, evaporated milk, etc.) **[Do you think milk is a healthy drink based on these results? Why or why not?]**

- **[What do you think of Kitten's family now?] [Do you think they care about her? Why or why not?]** (e.g., Well, they've left a big bowl of milk on the porch for her, so they must care about her.)

- **[What problems might occur for the family because they left the bowl of milk on the porch?]** Make a list of the possible problems. (e.g., Other animals might be attracted to the milk. The milk could be turned over by other animals, etc.)

- **[Do you think Kitten will venture out again looking for another "bowl of milk"? Why or why not?]** (See Writing section below.)

ACTIVITIES

The [ ] around the text indicate a question.

Writing

Have the children review their prior discussion of what they think Kitten has learned from her explorations. Have them create conversation bubbles about what advice she'd give. (See Resource section.) (e.g., Do you see that big "bowl of milk" in the sky? Don't try to get it, because you'll never reach it! I tried several times, and I ended up wet, tired, and hungry. I wish I had stayed home, drinking the sweet milk my owners gave me.)

- SAY: We talked earlier about how Kitten might feel when she finally decided to return home. She might feel happy, relieved, or experience a sense of relief with her decision to return home. **[Have you ever felt better after you stopped trying to do something that was impossible, or way too difficult, or that you just didn't like?]**

Have the children brainstorm various situations where they finally "released the struggle," and accepted the outcome. (e.g., I tried playing basketball, but I was just too short to be really good. I tried playing the piano, but I decided that I'd rather take gymnastics, etc.) Have the children copy one of the sentences or have them create their own sentence. Be available to help them sound out the words.

- Review the concept of adjectives. Explain that adjectives are words that describe things. Hold up a pencil and describe the qualities of the pencil. (e.g., It's long, thin, yellow, pointy, etc.) Make a list of adjectives describing Kitten's feelings. (e.g., Kitten might feel grateful, hungry, tired, happy, relieved, glad, etc.)

- Make a list of adjectives describing how Kitten's owners might feel. (e.g., relieved, curious, angry, happy, surprised, etc.)

Science

- **[Do you think Kitten's stomach could hold a lot of milk? Why or why not?]**

Go online and enter the question: How big is a cat's stomach? Read this information to the children. For a ten-pound cat, the stomach is approximately the size of a walnut. The human stomach is generally the size of a balled fist.

Math

Have the children predict whether Kitten will drink the entire bowl of milk. Graph their results. (e.g., Yes = 12, No = 13)

TEXT: just waiting for...

> **Direct the children's attention to the page where Kitten is drinking the milk on the porch. Encourage them to answer the following questions in complete sentences.**

The [ ] around the text indicate a question.

- **[What do you see in the picture?]**

- **[How do you think Kitten feels now?]** (See Art section below.)

- **[Do you think Kitten feels satisfied and content?] [Have you ever felt like this?]** Write the children's responses on a piece of paper. (See Writing section below.)

- **[Where do you think Kitten will spend the night?]**

- **[How do you think the family will react when they discover that Kitten has returned?]** (See Writing section below.)

- SAY: Today, animals can have a chip implanted in their body to locate them when they're lost. **[Does anyone have a pet that has this device?] [Do you think it's a good thing to have this device?]**

- **[If your animal got lost, what could you do to find her or him?]** Make a list of the various ways to find a pet. (e.g., A newspaper ad, posters in local stores, markets, recreational facilities, searches, etc.) Emphasize that safety is very important. You should never go searching for an animal alone.

- SAY: Kitten is just learning about her world. **[What precautions should the owners take to guarantee Kitten's safety?]** Make a list of possible things that she might need to be safe and happy. (e.g., Make sure all small objects are removed from the floor, so she doesn't swallow them. Make sure Kitten is supervised around other animals until they feel comfortable with her. Make sure she doesn't fall. Make sure young children are trained to carry her, etc.) **[What things could the family do to guarantee her well-being?]** (e.g., They could make sure she had a soft bed, a warm environment, clean eating containers, plenty of clean water, lots of healthy food, etc.)

- **[How is Kitten drinking her milk?]** (e.g., She's drinking the milk with her tongue.) Cats drink with their tongue, because it's natural for them. **[Do you think it would be difficult drinking with your tongue?]** (See Science section below.)

- SAY: A cat's tongue has little bumps on it. **[Why do you think they have these bumps on their tongue?]** (e.g., They grab the food and hold it on the tongue. The tongue also cleans their fur.)

Have a piece of sandpaper available for the children to feel. Explain to them that Kitten's tongue feels somewhat like a piece of sandpaper. (e.g., It has bumps or ridges that are rough.)

ACTIVITIES

The [ ] around the text indicate a question.

Art

Have the children illustrate this page, then cut out a tongue from a piece of pink felt or sandpaper. Glue the tongue to the illustration of Kitten.

Writing

- SAY: Kitten's family is probably glad that she's returned. Create a Welcome Back poster for Kitten. (e.g., Welcome Back Kitten! We're so happy that you came back home. You can have all the milk you can drink!)

- SAY: Earlier, we said that Kitten looked satisfied and content.

Have the children write one of the sentences from their list, or they can write their own sentence. Be available to help the children sound out the words.

Science

- SAY: Earlier, we discussed how Kitten drank the milk with her tongue. Today, we're going to see how that system works.

Have the children choose a partner to count the number of licks it takes to finish one tablespoon of water. Talk about appropriate behavior during this experiment. (e.g., Carefully lick the water off the plate. Be careful not to make sudden movements that could tip over the plate, etc.) Give each child one tablespoon of water on a plastic plate. Have the partner count the number of licks it took to finish the water. Record the number on a piece of paper. Do the same process for the partner.

- **[What observations would you make about this system?]**

- **[Did you each finish the water with the same number of licks?]**

- **[Why do you think this number was the same or different?]**

- **[What conclusions could you make about the prior experiment?]** (e.g., Well, licking water from a plate isn't easy. It would be easier to drink it from a glass. The number of licks might vary, so some of us were able to hold more water on our tongue than others. Drinking water from a glass is faster than licking the water from a plate.)

Math

Have the children practice writing and counting the number of licks it takes to finish the water.

TEXT: Lucky Kitten!

> **Direct the children's attention to the page where Kitten is asleep next to the bowl. Encourage them to answer the following questions in complete sentences.**

The [ ] around the text indicate a question.

- **[What do you see in the picture?]**

- SAY: Look carefully at the picture. **[What could you say about Kitten at this point?]** (e.g., She appears to be happy and satisfied.)

- **[What things does she have to be thankful for?]** Have the children make a list of these things. (e.g., She has a full tummy. She has a quiet place to sleep.)

- SAY: When bringing a new kitten into a home, it's important to make sure that it's a safe environment. Several things should be done before a kitten is introduced into the family. **[What should be done before a kitten is brought home?]**

Make a class list of things they think should be done before a new kitten is brought home. (e.g., Make sure that house plants are nontoxic. Make sure that small objects are removed from the floor to eliminate swallowing and choking. Make sure that young children are taught how to hold and carry a new kitten, etc.)

- SAY: Animals should wear a collar with an identification tag attached. Bring in a variety of different animal collars for the children to examine. Discuss the differences. (e.g., Some collars are wide, while others are thin. Some collars have designs on them, while others are plain, etc.) Create a beautiful new collar and identification tag for Kitten. (See Resource section.) (See Art section below.)

- SAY: Kitten had loving owners, but many animals don't have a loving home. **[How many of you have ever been to an animal shelter?]** Explain to the children that there are thousands of animals that need a home. Explain to them that there are procedures in place to adopt animals. These procedures protect the safety and well-being of the animals. Ask your local animal shelter if a representative could visit the class to explain what they do for these animals. Call the shelter in advance to find out what items can be donated and have the children bring these items to class. They should be collected before the shelter representative visits. (e.g., old towels, rags, blankets, etc.) If a representative can't visit the class, you could take the donated items to the shelter and relay to the staff that the children discussed the value of the shelter and they personally collected the items. Ask them if they have any informational brochures that could be read in class. Perhaps the shelter could provide the children with brochures to take home. (See Writing section below.)

- Perhaps the children would like to have an animal shelter fundraiser, where the money raised would be donated to their local shelter. The class should brainstorm ways that the money could be raised, and then decide how they should proceed. (e.g., Selling pencils, selling animal stickers, having their picture taken with a pet, having a lunch-time movie, or distributing an animal protection bucket to each class, etc.)

Have a class discussion about how they should spend the money they earn from the fundraiser. Make a class list of spending possibilities. If the animal shelter staff feels that specific items are needed, relay what they've requested. It allows the children an opportunity to give something to their community that is truly needed.

- The author ends this story with Kitten falling asleep near her bowl, with the text, "Lucky Kitten!"

- **[If you could end this story, how would you end it?]** Draw and write an alternative ending to this story. (See Writing section below.)

- The last page shows Kitten asleep near her bowl. The text says, "Lucky Kitten!" Have the class create an acrostic poem with these words. (See Writing section below.)

- **[Why was Kitten lucky?]** Write the children's responses on a piece of paper. (e.g., She was lucky because she wasn't hurt during the night. She was lucky because she didn't get chased by other animals. She was lucky because she remembered how to get home, etc.)

ACTIVITIES

The [ ] around the text indicate a question.

Art

- SAY: Kitten returned to her home, however, some animals get lost. **[What could be done to prevent Kitten from being lost?]** (e.g., When an animal is old enough to go outside, it should have some type of identification.) **[Do you think it would be a good idea for Kitten to have an identification tag?]** Hold up an identification tag for the children to see. Tell the children you're going to make an identification tag for Kitten, but if they'd like to make a tag for their pet, that would be fine. Give each child a piece of poster board. On a separate piece of paper, have them draw various shapes they'd like to consider for the tag. (e.g., a bell, a moon, a bowl, a flower, a firefly, etc.) Have the children decide what shape they want and carefully draw the shape onto the poster board. Tell them it should be large enough to write the important facts about the animal. (e.g., "Kitten," 598-498-1757.) Have them color the tag. (See Resource section.)

Tell the children they're going to make a beautiful new collar for Kitten. If the children would prefer, they could make the collar for their own pet. Cut pieces of poster board into long strips. Punch holes at both ends. Allow the children to draw, paint, or glue special items onto the collar, creating a unique design. They could use stickers, dried flowers, studs, sequins, moons, stars, etc. Allow the collar to dry, and then tie yarn, twine, or ribbon to both ends of the collar. Emphasize to the children that their collar is just for fun, not something that would be tied around their pet's neck. The children could attach the identification tag they made earlier to the new collar. Display the collars on a bulletin board.

Writing

- SAY: Animal shelters distribute information to the public about the services they offer. Create an informational brochure about their local animal shelter. Bring in a variety of different business brochures, so the children can view and discuss the important features of the brochure. (e.g., Where the organization is located. What the organization does. The value of the organization to the community, etc.)

As a group, create an animal shelter brochure on a piece of paper, then allow the children to create their own. Be available to help them sound out the words.

- SAY: The author ended the story with the text, "Lucky Kitten!" **[How would you end the story?]** Make a class list of possible alternative endings. (e.g., Kitten wakes up and searches for more food. Kitten thinks that there's a tall tree on the next block that might get her closer to that bowl of milk. Kitten decided that she'd rather have canned food rather than more milk, etc.) Have the children write and draw one of the endings listed or write their own ending. Be available to help the children sound out the words.

- Create an acrostic poem with the class, using the ending line in the book that reads, "Lucky Kitten!" Review the reasons why Kitten was lucky. Have the children copy the class poem or create their own poem. (See example.)

L - Licking her paw in the field at night,

U - Under the bright, full moon.

C - Catching fireflies on her tongue,

K - Keeping her sights set on that bowl of milk.

Y - Yum, yum, she will taste it soon.

K

I

T   etc.

T

E

N

ABOUT THE AUTHOR

Claudia Krause was a public school teacher for nearly twenty years, while simultaneously tutoring various academic subjects at a commercial tutoring center. She has published a book with Simon Schuster, who distributed her work to teachers throughout the United States. She has a Bachelor's Degree in Psychology from California State University, at Long Beach, California, and a Master's Degree in Education from Redlands University, at Redlands, California. She has one daughter, who lives on the East Coast and two grandsons. She enjoys traveling to various locations and obtaining cultural, historical, and educational information that can be incorporated into her works.

LOOK FOR THE NEXT CALDECOTT ACTIVITY BOOK COMING SOON!

Grandfather's Journey, by Allen Say

This is a story about a grandfather who leaves Japan to see the world.

1994 Caldecott Medal Winner

Here are some examples of upcoming activities that you'll see in the book.

Have the children bring in pictures of their grandfathers as they appeared when they were young men. Put a present-day picture below the earlier picture of them as they appeared as young men. Put these pictures on a bulletin board. If they are unable to obtain a picture of their grandfather, have them bring in a picture of an older person they admire.

Have the children interview their grandfather. If possible, invite the grandfathers to class to relay some information about their lives. This can be accomplished over several days. If interviewing the grandfather isn't possible, have the children interview an older man they admire.

- The author tells us that the grandfather left his home in Japan. Locate Japan on a world map and calculate the distance from their home to Japan. Show a world map and talk about *scale*.

- Look carefully at the picture showing Grandfather wearing traditional Japanese clothing. Discuss various kinds of clothing worn throughout the world. Ask the children if anyone in their family has clothing like this. Invite them to bring it to class. If no one has clothing like this, go online and research traditional Japanese clothing.

- This book is beautifully illustrated. Allow the children to choose a page from the book that they'd like to illustrate. Give each child a set of watercolors or paints and a sheet of good drawing paper. Display the finished illustrations on a bulletin board.

- The author tells us that Grandfather traveled on a steamship. Have the children research steamships/steamboats. Have them determine how long it would take to get from Japan to North America.

If you enjoyed this Caldecott Activity Book, I'd love to send you two free pages of Activities and Questions from the pre-publication edition of the next Caldecott Activity Book. It will be used in conjunction with Grandfather's Journey, by Allen Say. I'll send the material to you as quickly as possible. If you enjoyed this book, I'd love to have you send me a review.

SEND YOUR NAME, ADDRESS,
AND EMAIL TO ME AT MY WEB ADDRESS:
krause_claudia@hotmail.com

RESOURCES

Moon

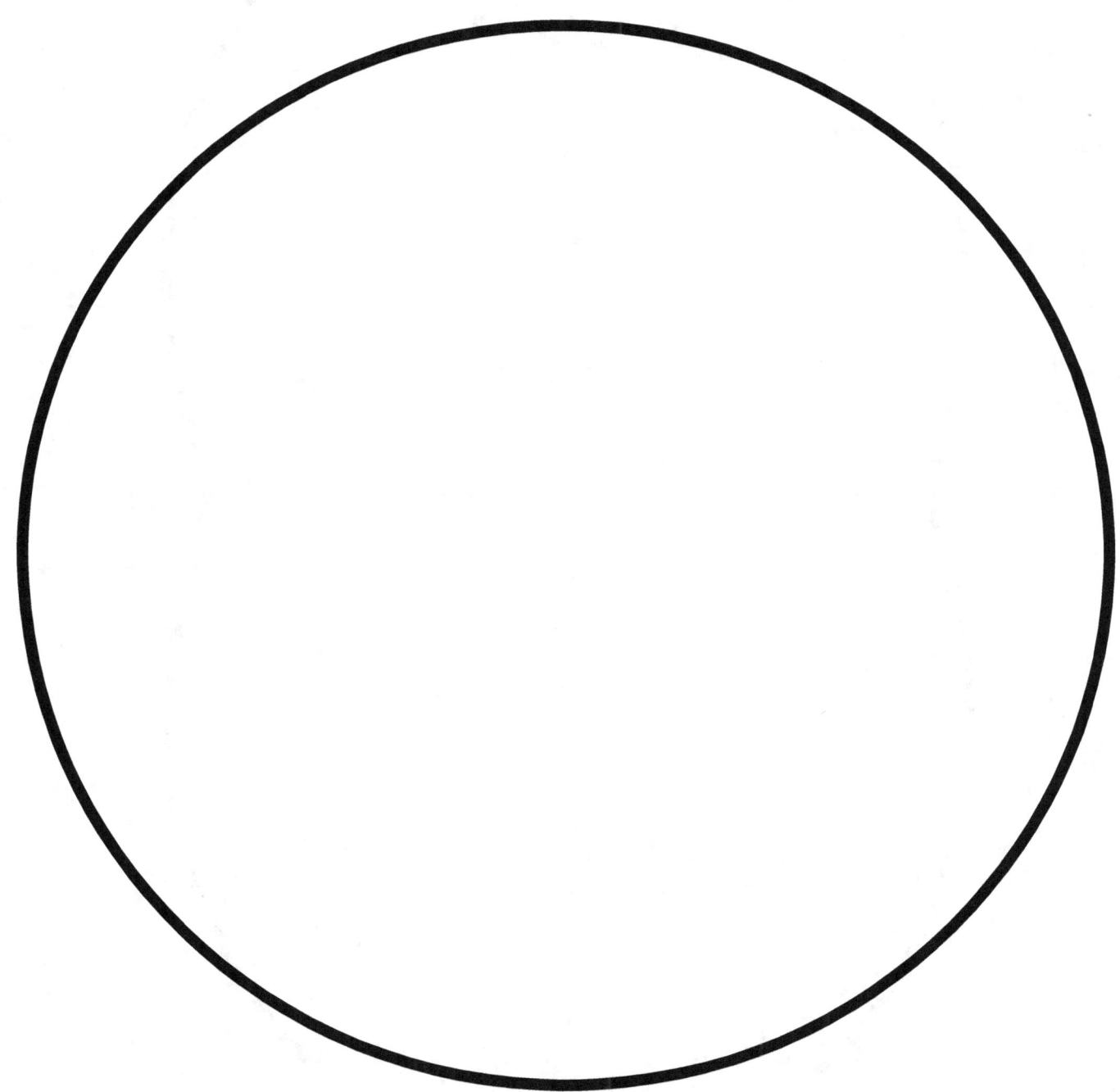

Tongue

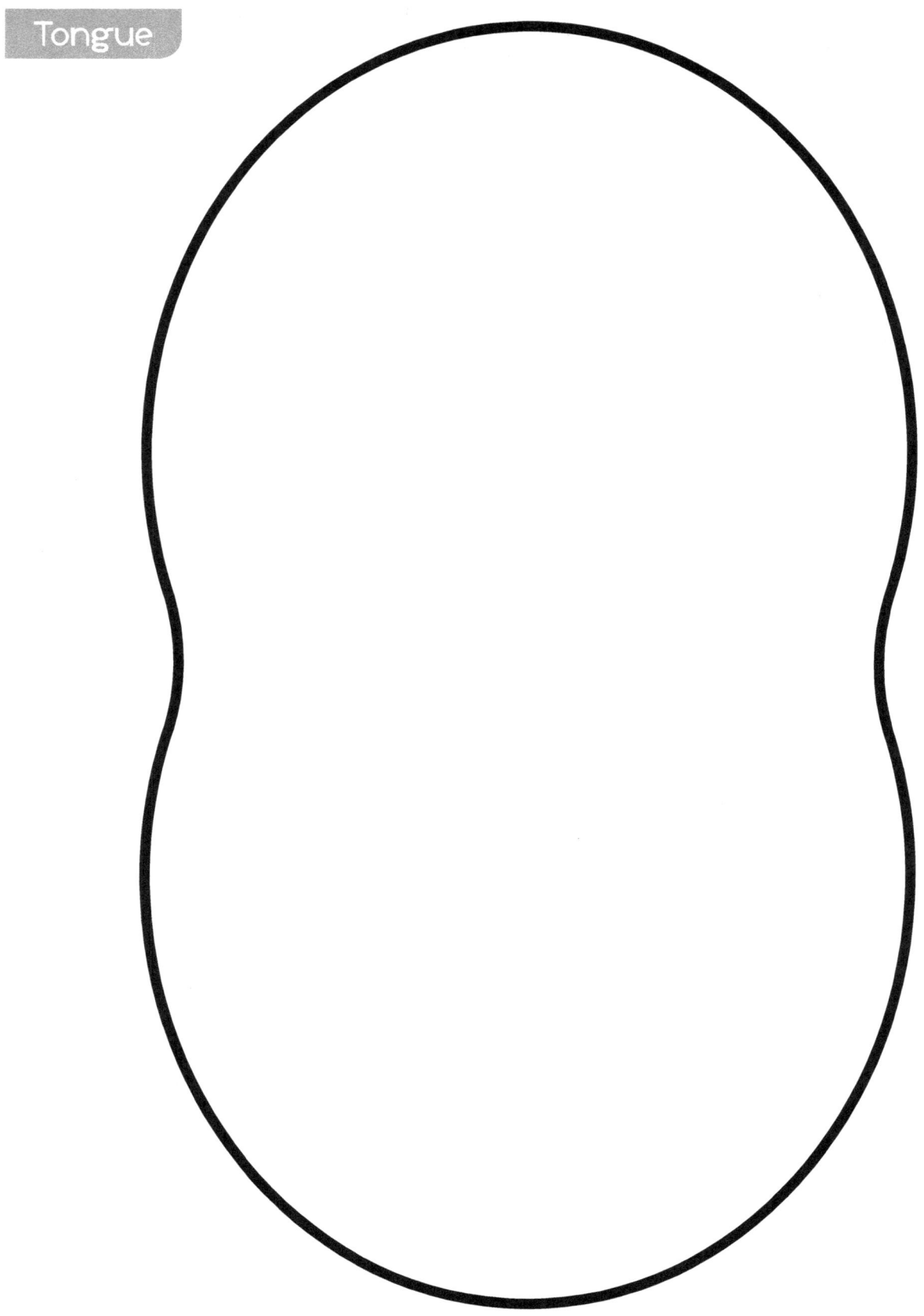

Permission Slip

Dear Parent(s),

Our class will be learning about the taste areas on our tongue. We'll be tasting sweet (sugar), sour (lemon), salty (salt), bitter (coffee), and savory substances (soy sauce or crushed tomatoes.) Please mark which permission you give, and then sign the form at the bottom of the page. Please return it to school as soon as possible. Your child will not be allowed to participate in this science experiment without this permission form. Thank you in advance for completing and returning the form.

_____I give permission for my child to taste all the substances listed above.

_____I give permission for my child to taste the above substances EXCEPT_____.
(Write in which substance(s) you do not want your child to taste.)

_____I do not give permission for my child to taste any of the substances listed above.

_____

Parent signature

Rocket Top

62

Clock Back

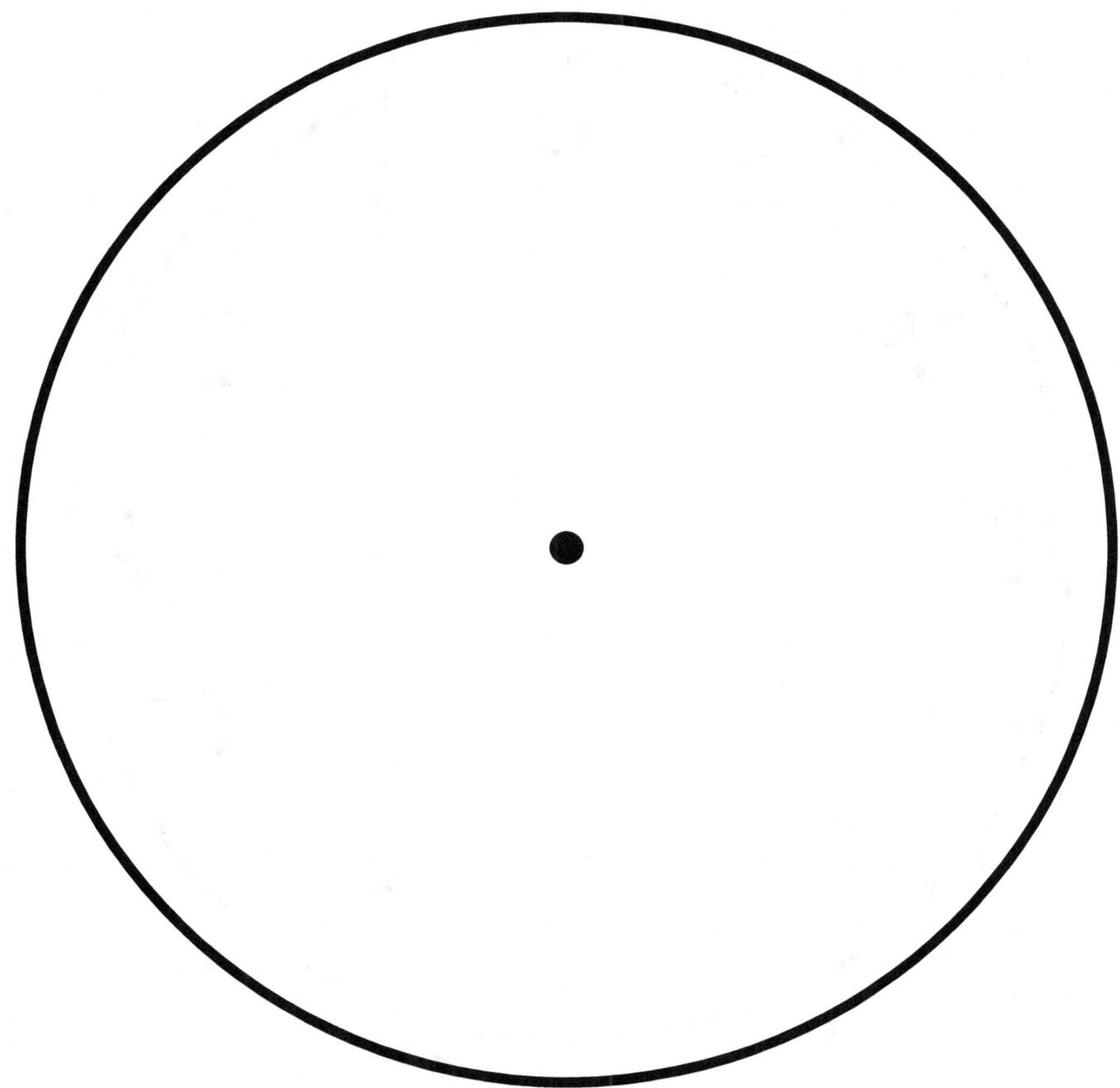

Clock Face

Identification Tag Examples

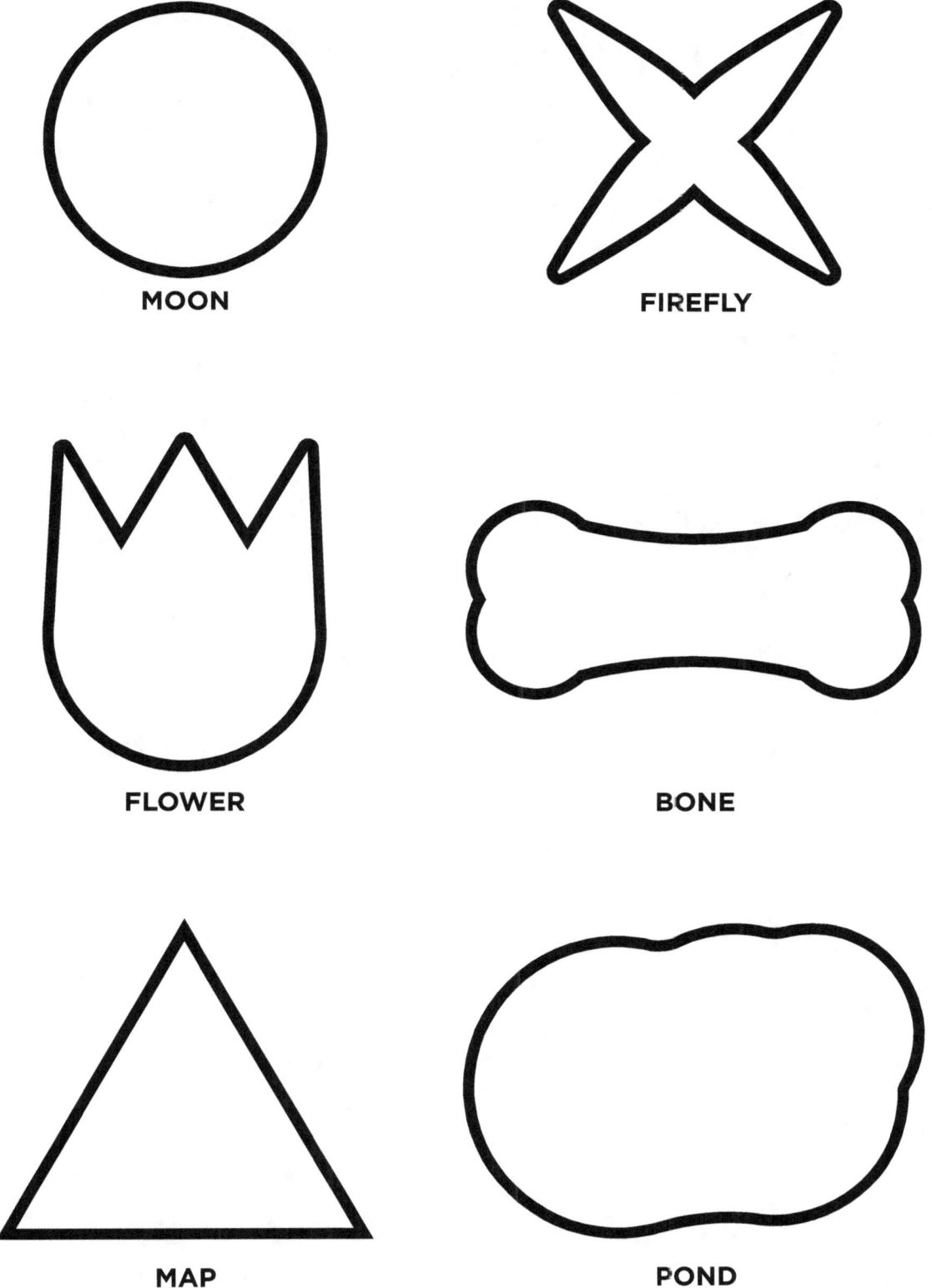

What I Know About Cats	What I Want To Know About Cats	What I Learned About Cats
• I know cats have ears. • I know cats have claws.	• I want to know if cats have good hearing. • I want to know if cats have a good sense of smell.	• There are many different types of cats.

Samples

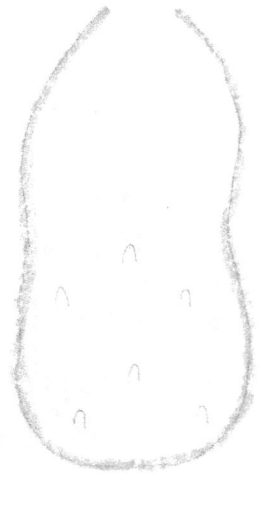

Tongue

Samples

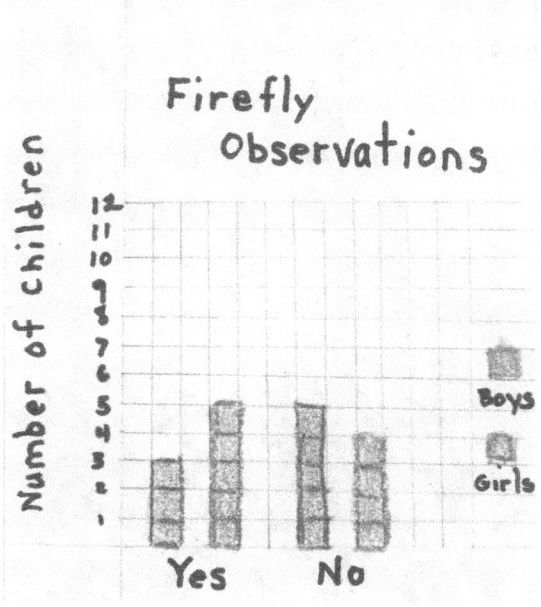

Fireflies

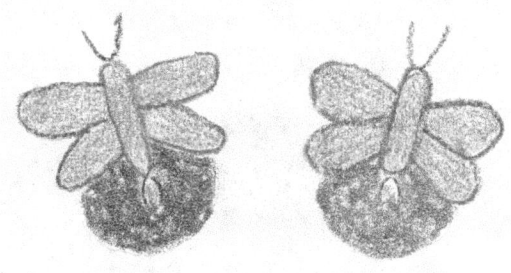

Firefly on Kitten's Tongue

Samples

Samples

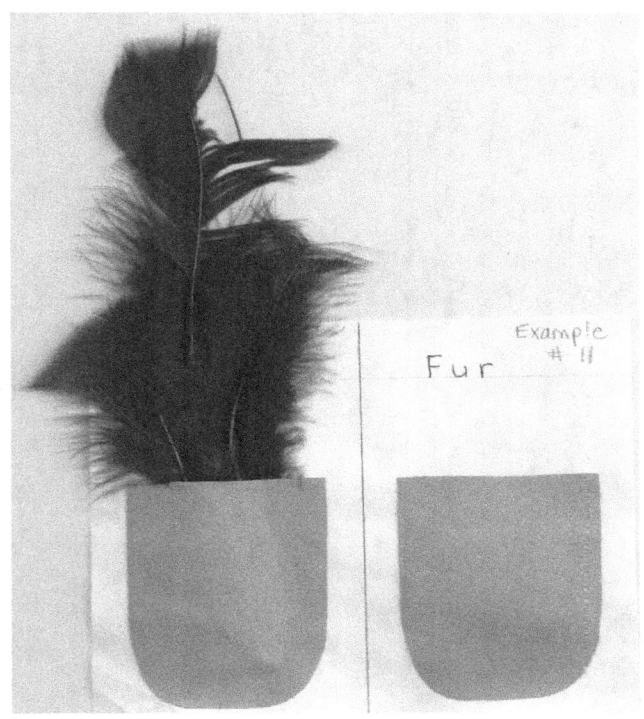

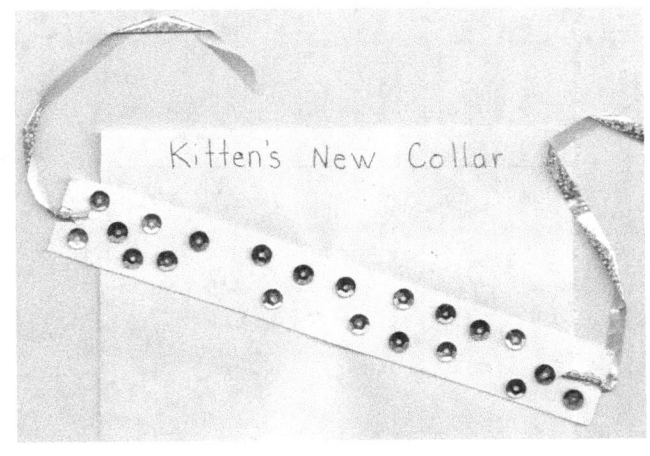

Acknowledgments

To all who contributed to this book in any form, I'm deeply grateful. I'd especially like to thank the staff at 1106 Design in Phoenix, Arizona for their direction and guidance. They were instrumental in guiding me through the myriad steps it took to complete this book.

www.ingramcontent.com/pod-product-compliance
Lightning Source LLC
Chambersburg PA
CBHW051422070526
44584CB00023B/3545